T0358705

Teaching Writing While Standing on One Foot

Teaching Writing While Standing on One Foot

Robert Danberg

Binghamton University, USA

SENSE PUBLISHERS
ROTTERDAM/BOSTON/TAIPEI

A C.I.P. record for this book is available from the Library of Congress.

ISBN: 978-94-6300-113-7 (paperback)
ISBN: 978-94-6300-114-4 (hardback)
ISBN: 978-94-6300-115-1 (e-book)

Published by: Sense Publishers,
P.O. Box 21858,
3001 AW Rotterdam,
The Netherlands
https://www.sensepublishers.com/

Printed on acid-free paper

For Anne Sklov
"A book in the family wouldn't be such a bad thing".

TABLE OF CONTENTS

ACKNOWLEDGEMENTS

My son Rubin and daughter Goldali, who lived with its writing and inspired its completion. They are behind every page.

My parents, Kenneth and Gail Danberg, my brothers, Ira Danberg and David Danberg, and sister, Elana Danberg Brody, who always asked "How is the book going?" and kept faith.

Jessica Doerr and Rachel Buff, who have been an "ever-fixed mark" for me for many, many years.

Thomas Girshin and Esty Shachter, who read drafts and whose comments helped me understand what I had to say.

Paul Shovlin, who reminded me to write in the way I'd written about my grandmother.

Louise Wetherbee Phelps, Antonio diRenzo, Nance Hahn, Bob Stein, Riv-Ellen Prell, Maria Damon, Denise Johnson, Kurt Spellmeyer, Thomas Lux, Kate Johnson and Robin Brown—all teachers who appeared at just the right moments.

Brian, Josh, Ron, Cathrene, Jerry, and all of the other friends on the path.

Robert Lake and Tricia Kress for the opportunity to write this book.

Marc Dennis for his encouragement.

Jaya Lalita for wise counsel.

Karin Suskin for help beyond measure.

Cover Photograph by Stiller Zussman. Feet by Rubin, Goldali, Laila, and the author.

"Something for Nothing: The Writing Teacher's Work" originally appeared in Writing on the Edge, Spring 2012.

TEACHING WRITING WHILE STANDING ON ONE FOOT

1

When people ask me what I do, I always say "I'm a writing teacher." I say "writing teacher" for the same reason that when I was a kid and people asked me what my father did, I'd say "He's in the garment industry." Like the garment industry for my father, the classrooms, colleagues, and students involved in the business of teaching and learning writing make up a culture built around a purpose: teaching and learning writing. I've taught freshman composition and basic writing classes, GED classes, adult education in "welfare to work" programs, and English as a Second Language classes in a jobs program for recent immigrants. I've taught adults to read and helped dissertation writers get started (or finish). In the last ten years, I've taught academic writing and workplace writing. I've also trained teachers. I've taught writing in large and small colleges, four-year and community colleges, private and public institutions. "Writing" hasn't always meant the same thing. It could mean a grocery list, a letter home, a book report, a college essay, or a dissertation. Or at least, that's what writing means when classes begin. If the work goes well, by the end of class, "writing" will become a way: "a way to say what I what I want to say in the words I want to use" and "a way to discover what I think and feel" and "a way to know and remember." Whether the student is a seventy-year-old woman making her first written sentence into her first story, an adult returning to college after struggling to write her first paper, an eighteen-year-old in freshman writing class, or a stumped dissertation writer, it's always the same: "writing" begins as a thing and ends as a way.

Despite the ostensible differences in the subject matter of those classes, the students have been similar in ways as important as the ways they were different. College writers come in as experts on what high school requires and then have to learn what a professor wants. Workplace writing students are experts on what professors want and have to learn what a boss expects. Graduate students have to learn to make dissertations, a genre that thrives in one habitat only, the graduate school. Then they have to learn how to write for a professional public.

The literacy students want to learn to read the words they know, but also learn how to read words they may have never heard spoken. The students I've taught often come to class and rely on a narrow set of strategies that worked for them in the past and now work against them. Adult literacy students often equate reading with pronunciation. Reading becomes laborious and frustrating when the primary strategy for coping with an unfamiliar word is to sound it out syllable by syllable. She may stall over at a word and ignore context clues that might help her.

Many college students spend an inordinate amount of time on the first paragraph of an essay. They tell me that once they figure out the first paragraph, they know what to say. Then, they go on to write the paper, and as they write, learn more about what they want to say, and then never return to the opening, even though that opening no longer pertains to the essay they wanted to write. The last paragraph they write, the one they call the conclusion, often turns out to make a good beginning. When they try to write the opening paragraph before writing much else, they try to do two very different things at once that work at cross purposes: discovering what they mean, and crafting a rhetorical strategy that will hook a reader. Figuring out what they mean requires a maximal approach to making pages; to figure out the best way to bring a reader into a piece, a writer labors over a few sentences that take only a few seconds of a reader's time. All the students I've met, new reader to dissertation writer share misconceptions about what "good writers" do, and these misconceptions become convictions that hobble them. They believe good writers require few drafts. They believe good writers don't solicit the feedback of friends and colleagues. They believe good writers don't have to plan or rewrite. Many of these beliefs stem from the fact that we learn to write under performance conditions. When we practice writing in grade school, middle school, and high school, we are graded.

When I tell people I'm a college writing teacher, they often ask me if my students write "worse" than they did when I began teaching. By "worse" they mean "Are your students' spelling, grammar, and punctuation worse than they were twenty-five years ago?" and "Why can't they write sentences that make sense?" Many people confide in me that they can't write. They say that they labor over even the briefest workplace email. Some confess that they hated classes like mine and resented them, but occasionally some say how important the class turned out to be.

Some tell me how much they love to write. They might not write much now but they used to write poems or keep a journal. A few tell me they keep diaries. The most common story I hear is about the time they felt hurt or shamed by a teacher or a friend they shared their writing with. They thought that person would like it, or they believed they were done and were happy with it, or they just wanted someone to read it. I understand. There was that time in Ms. Johnson's twelfth grade AP English class when I worked so hard and felt such a deep need to impress her that I volunteered for her to read my paper aloud. I remember the precise sentence when the class burst out laughing, and where I was sitting, and the hot shame. There was that time I gave my favorite professor a sheaf of poems and he said—well, it doesn't matter. I also remember the careless, arrogant thing I said to my friend Jessica almost thirty years ago. I remember her hurt and anger so well that I can remember exactly where we were and what time of night it was and what I said. My casual dismissal of her writing embarrasses me almost as much as anything has ever embarrassed me.

So when I teach, I always remember: *At least cause no shame.*

I hear a lot about frustration with other people's writing. A food scientist I sit next to at my son's Little League games works at a laboratory that tests food products for snack companies. She describes what happens when a freshly minted PhD, a young scientist, submits his first memos and reports. She says these new hires write their reports as if the goal is to express what they think or to produce an academic essay rather than to communicate findings. My brother complains about lengthy emails and verbose memos that he needs to cut and turn around for revision. He wants bulleted lists, concise sentences, and short paragraphs.

What frustrates my friend and my brother most is that they find themselves showing people what they think those people should already know. I asked them how they handled their frustration. The food scientist reviews those first reports sentence by sentence and meets with the employee. She explains how the report she wants differs from the one the new employee submitted. My brother tells his employees what he wants and demonstrates what he expects. Each of them steps into an employee's writing life at a moment when direct instruction from an experienced writer matters most, when learning from experience is impossible to avoid, and when learning to write matters.

I've told my friend and my brother that they are excellent teachers. Respectful and direct, they intervene precisely when help is needed. Those are the moments when instruction makes the most sense. Writing teachers work hard to create these moments in the classroom. I've heard complaints like my friend's and my brother's from colleagues as well. They are baffled by weak thesis statements, sentences containing basic errors of expression, and organizational schemes that fail at the level of the paragraph and the paper. As often as I've heard colleagues dismiss students and their writing, I've heard colleagues—not writing teachers, but teachers in disciplines like history, philosophy, and the sciences—tell me how they've made changes in their classes to encourage the writing they'd like to read. They've changed their approaches to writing and how they express their assignments. One history teacher devotes class periods in a junior seminar to going over the style she expects and how to rewrite for it. But whether the teacher believes she has a role to play in her students' writing or she dismisses their writing as beyond help, the lament is the same: they have to teach what students should know already, and what's worse, the students don't know they don't know or don't seem to care.

These students are *my* students. My class is the class that teaches "writing" to the people who go on to work for my brother and friend and take courses with my colleagues. But I wonder if what is missing is something else. Although some might not know or care, perhaps it's not that these students don't know how to produce what their teachers expect. They don't use what they know or don't pay enough attention to what they don't know.

Every writing course answers the question, "What does a writer know?" Sometimes I tell students that writers have two kinds of knowledge, stuff I can tell them and stuff they can only learn for themselves. This book concerns the stuff they can only learn for themselves. By that I don't mean the development of skill through practice, although that is part of what I mean, since the knowledge I have in mind is often only evident in the act of writing itself. Writers show what they understand by writing, not through formal responses to direct questions. For example, say I insist to my students that rhetorical analysis is crucial to writing successfully. When I assign them an essay, I give them a handout that asks them to answer questions about the audience for the piece, their stance with respect to that audience, the subject matter, the writing context, and the purpose of the essay. Many students will be able to answer those questions. Only a few students will show that they understand them in the essay they submit. Sometimes we call that stuff intuitive knowledge or experiential knowledge. It's what we mean when we say "eye" or "ear" or "feel."

This kind of knowledge presents a particular challenge to me as a writing teacher. Often this knowledge is only available to the student through the act of writing itself. It's immune to direct instruction, although I can describe it or gesture towards it. In fact, gestures are often the most efficient form of direct instruction available to a writing teacher. I can always tell when someone has begun to experience writing as a journey toward clarity that begins in uncertainty, rather than the reproduction of models or adherence to rules of correctness in response to a direct question. She leans into the page between us like she's trying to find something she knows is there. When I point to a sentence, her eyes go there. Then she takes the paper back and turns to a passage to show me what I've missed and explains her plan.

Students are often confused about this aspect of a writer's knowledge. They crave rules and recipes. Yet, many have been enriched by the practice of creation, often privately, away from school, from home, on the field, in the studio, in the kitchen, among friends. They recognize the complex interplay between rehearsal and performance, practice and game when the subject is the next concert or the next meet, but set aside what they know about this kind of learning when the subject is writing. Their early encounters with writing and drawing seem to be all rehearsal and play, but by the time students reach high school, we've spent most our schooling in writing trying to "get it right," often uncertain what our teachers mean by "right" or even what "it" is supposed to be. How many of us could learn to hit a baseball if they only practiced during games, when the pitcher's goal is to strike them out? To acquire the kind of knowledge I am trying to describe here, writers must fail. Good teachers create the likelihood of failure and good classrooms create the conditions for failure so that later, all of what the writer has been told and practiced flows into a single moment of contact.

Sometimes, people describe this kind of knowledge by saying they want their students to "Think like." I asked a biologist what she hoped the non-majors who took "Introduction to Biology" took away from the class. She answered me with a story. A former "Intro" student picks up the *Pennysaver* in her hometown grocery store. She flips to the Letters to the Editor and reads a letter claiming that global warming does not exist. The letter writer bases her claim on a study she read about which shows that global temperatures haven't changed significantly over the last ten years. Instead of "Wow, I didn't know that," the biologist wants her student to think: "Is ten years enough time to make a claims about the existence of global warming?" My colleague wants her former student in some modest way to think like a scientist, which in this case means that when her student hears a claim based on a study, she asks the study's sample size, methods, and relevance to the claim.

A student doesn't have to become a scientist to learn how scientists think, nor does she need to be a scientist to think like one. But, when we say someone thinks like a biologist, a historian, or a writer, we mean something in addition to what that person knows about taxonomy, the Louisiana Purchase, or the difference between an informal and an academic style. We recognize in her actions a constellation of attributes that includes what she sees, feels and knows. When we say someone thinks like a writer, we expect her to sense what a writer senses, attend to what a writer attends to, and feel a certain kind of urgency that comes when a writer looks for the right way to say what she means. We also mean that she behaves like a writer behaves when confronted with a particular problem or situation. She recognizes when she needs to use what she knows and uses that knowledge. Often, when we say someone thinks like a biologist or an historian or a writer, we mark what she has *begun* to do. A biologist would never say it of another biologist. But when she observes a student making assured and skillful choices or asking certain questions or speculating in specific way, essentially demonstrating behavior characteristic of a scientist, she might say to her student, "Now you're thinking like a scientist."

When people try to explain how teachers don't teach students what students need to know, they tend to emphasize a failure to transmit knowledge, not a failure to create situations through which students can acquire "the stuff we can't tell them." We know what the elements of good writing look like. We have handbooks full of instructions, tips, examples, rules, and strategies. We can show models, make corrections, demonstrate, lecture, and assess. We can organize knowledge into hierarchies that lead students from the 'building blocks' on to complex edifices, or de-engineer complex edifices so that we can regard their components. Since we can compare a student's essays and processes to our models of them, we ought to be able to trace what is missing back to a place in instruction where that missing piece can be found, then tell the student what she ought to have done instead.

In school, we watch how others succeed and fail. We come to know our successes, failures, limitations, and habits. That intimacy with our own failures and successes humbles some of us and makes others of experts in what humbles others.

But we rarely have a complete grasp of how we learned to read and write. We remember what makes an impression on us. What we remember, I think, are the times we were told something or when something was demonstrated to us, perhaps on a blackboard, or shown to us in a book. We remember the moment we demonstrated command, which might come at the end of a long, vaguely understood process. I remember the fold-out bed in the living room where my mother read *One Fish Two Fish Red Fish Blue Fish* to me and my younger brother.

I know I couldn't have been older than five, and I might have been as young as four. Many people identify those moments of competence with the process of learning itself.

While we often neglect to account for knowledge that only shows itself through the act of creation, we recognize it and have ways of talking about it. Eliot Eisner, the noted philosopher of education, observes that we praise a uniquely talented chef, mechanic, or teacher by calling her an *artist*. When we call a plumber or a doctor an artist, we look past the craft to the situations that face them and what they make of them. A physician recognizes symptoms that she cannot associate with a familiar disease. A mechanical engineer designs a structure he must invent tools to build. An arithmetic teacher, listening to a child's question, tries to figure out what her student's confusion says about what her student understands.

The students who take my writing classes do not come as artists-to-be. Some of my students may become writers, in the sense that they may write poetry or screenplays or technical manuals or grants. Almost all will become something other than writers. Some may want make something beautiful from words, but most simply wish to make something true out of them, and by true, I mean in the way a carpenter planes a door so that it swings in the door frame. For the purposes of my First Year Writing Class or Introduction to Professional Writing class, I define a writer as someone who makes things with words in a way that shows skill, intelligence, and sense of form. She needs to be flexible, sensitive to the demands of a situation, able to adapt what she knows to new demands, eager to learn as she goes. The competent writer produces what a situation calls for and she corrects her course based on the feedback she receives. And she consistently produces well organized writing, free of lapses in correctness.

Interestingly, while it's common to say "my mechanic is a real artist," it's equally as common to hear artists use some form of the verb *to make* when they describe how they created something. For example, I hear painters say they *made a picture*, rather than *painted a painting*. I've heard Peter Martins, the choreographer and dancer, and Robert Wilson, the theatre artist, describe how they *made* a dance. When we identify expertise with artistry we call attention to finesse, ingenuity, or skillfulness. When a painter, dancer, or poet calls himself or herself a *maker*, what does she mean us to pay attention to? Work, mostly. Tools, materials, rehearsal, practice. When an artist uses some form of the verb *to make,* she shifts our attention from the apparent mysteries of inspiration to the work of the studio or the rehearsal hall where things are tried and cast off; where tables, walls, and floors are scattered, hung, and littered with ideas.

When the artist calls herself a *maker*, she's thinking of the tried and true, the craft she's come to rely on that allows her to cope with the uncertainty of creation. She's talking about mere work. But work is the path through which students will acquire the knowledge they need to learn to think like writers. It's through work with materials that artists discover, clarify, and come to understand the piece they want to create. Writing classes appear to be organized around activities, themes, genres, readings, and revision, but they are really organized around work with materials. We teach our students how to do their work. Work with materials can seem like a loose collection of discrete activities. All that problem solving, analysis, drafting, and revising gathered into a rough process defined as a beginning, middle, and end is usually assigned according to what the calendar demands and not necessarily the internal energy of the project. Simply put, you can never really say in a writing class, *I'm not done yet.* Part of what a writer needs to learn is how to be done when she needs to be. By working with materials, students learn how and when a technique might be useful, how to orchestrate a process of discovery, and how to adapt common procedures to new and unique demands. Every solution that fails provides the student with an alternative.

When we distinguish a technically competent writer from one whose work is skillful and imaginative, we don't point to how well the writer adheres to rules and standards. A "technically" perfect performance is often considered weak when compared to one that is skillful and imaginative but technically weaker. I once tutored two servicemen who were struggling in school. One had been a private, a clerk. He described how until college "writing" meant filling out reports based on information he'd been given. Essentially, he completed forms. It's likely there were many kinds of forms. Army bureaucracy can ship thousands of soldiers and tons of equipment around the world in hours. As he explained it, however, completing these forms was a simple routine. The second student was an officer at work on a master's degree. His writing had been more elaborate and more a product of his own insights and observations, but he was clear that the writing he did was also a kind of form. From the way they explained their work in the past and what they didn't know how to do now, they struck me as thoughtful writers.

Sometimes students come to class expressing a wish for a recipe, rule, or method. They picture a writer's knowledge organized like the handbooks they are required to buy but rarely consult. Perhaps unconsciously they imagine that a writer recognizes a situation, then searches for the appropriate response the way I always consult the Fannie Farmer Cookbook when I want to make cookies, even though I've made them many times before. Or maybe they picture a long list of instructions that they can take up one element at a time. It may be that since these soldiers were in their thirties or forties when they returned to school, they understood that while there was much I could teach them, the information I could offer was limited. They knew that they need to be flexible, open to change, and willing to adapt. They needed knowledge about conventions, and instruction in craft, but they also needed the kinds of knowledge they could only acquire—or even become aware of—through experience. Without that knowledge all those rules and forms and procedures would be like a string of lights with one dead bulb.

Insight often begins with confusion and disappointment. There is an old Jewish legend about the necessity for uncertainty when it comes to learning something for ourselves.

One day, a nonbeliever approaches the great sage Shammai.

"Teach me the whole of Torah while I stand on one foot, and I'll convert."

Shammai chases him off with a carpenter's rod, a sturdy measuring stick one cubit long. If you want to build an ark like Noah, you need a cubit-long carpenter's rod.

Next, the nonbeliever approaches the great sage Hillel.

"Teach me the whole of the Torah while I stand on one foot."

That's when Hillel utters the line that makes the legend famous: "That which is hateful to you do not do to others. The rest is commentary; go and learn it."

A friend who practices yoga tells me that in yoga, standing on one foot is a posture of balance and stability. But in this story—and this is why it appeals to me as a writing teacher—standing on one foot evokes instability. The lesson is over before the nonbeliever has barely been on one foot. Unknowingly, he puts himself at risk to learn. Many students come to writing class like the nonbeliever: they dare me to teach them. But a successful writing class persuades students to put themselves at risk to learn. It's hard to take on the role of a beginner. Yet I know from experience that learning anything when I am unwilling to take on risk, I improve the least. When I'm attached to the way I've done things, or am unwilling to revise a particular lesson, rule or principle I've followed in the past, I stand my ground. But it's a small patch of ground. When a student believes she has no ground to defend, all the ground is hers. The act of writing is no longer her adversary. When a student tells me how stressful it is to figure out what to write, or how unsure she is of where to start or which idea to choose, or is worried that no matter what she does, it will be wrong, I always answer, "You're so lucky. Why don't you just make a strong choice, do what you think, and then we'll have something to discuss." Or when the student comes to class and says she didn't do last night's writing because she wasn't sure what she was supposed to do, I say "The only wrong answer is not to give an answer. Make a strong choice and commit." Or a fretful student might tell me that she has no idea what to do, as if she's made out of wrong answers, and I say, " That's not a problem, that's writing. Welcome to the tribe."

Another friend admitted to me that for years she thought Hillel was supposed to stand on one foot, not the student. That misreading appeals to me, too. In writing class, I often find myself facing my students on one foot. A writing class is only an idea about what writers need to know until everyone shows up. When what a writer learns depends on doing work, knowledge appears when she writes. What she does defines her as much as what she knows. When I listen to my brother, my friends, and my colleagues, I wonder if the problem isn't that their employees and students don't know what they need to do, it's that they don't use what they know; or perhaps they don't even recognize that there is something to learn.

Many of my students come to class believing that writing starts when they open a file on their computers and begin the first paragraph. However, I know it will be easier for them in the long run if I show them other ways to find material that can help them think and plan. There are drafts, but there can also be models, storyboards, and journal entries that trigger insights and advance the process. Sometimes students ask me where good ideas come from; I think they should be asking *when* do ideas come.

I stand on one foot in front of the class sure of the choices I've made, but uncertain about the ones they will make. There's that moment when I read their drafts and get a familiar sinking feeling. A whole month organized around the production of this draft: instruction, practice, reflection, time to write, time to talk, time to reflect. And…this. Even thought I know what to expect, I always wonder: Have the choices I've made been good ones, Will the student's work *get better*? Can I make a difference? What is the right word to say? The right note to give? When should I ask questions? When should I just tell the student, "Do this. Move this paragraph here and see what happens."

In a letter to Martin Buber, the great Jewish philosopher and educator Franz Rosenzweig observed that our attention usually goes to the first part: *That which is hateful to you do not do to others.* But Rosenzweig thought the second part held the key. Hillel doesn't mean, "The rest is only commentary." To simply follow precepts is not to know, or at least not to entirely know, Torah.

To know Torah is to know the lesson, but also to participate in an ongoing conversation, an inquiry really, into the lesson's value.

Writing classes are full of lessons, rules, principles and resources, methods and handbooks, but they teach the commentary.

COMMENTARY: TELL THE STORY OF YOUR LIFE AS A WRITER

Tell the story of your life as a writer.

Complete it in one sitting.
Choose a length of time you instantly feel is "too short."
Do not exceed a half an hour.
Include "everything."
Interpret "everything" to include "anything."
No matter where you are in the last five minutes, end in the present.
Tell it backwards.

ENFOLDED KNOWLEDGE

1

At around six years old, when it became clear that baseball would be the interest that would outlast fire fighting in my son's life, I had nothing to teach him. I never watched baseball. I never had a favorite team. I did my time in Little League, and never, if I could help it, picked up a baseball again. So, I did what I often do when I don't know how to do something; I went to the library.

My son took charge of his learning from the beginning. At first, we played catch. I didn't own a glove, so when he began to throw hard, he contrived to get me one. We stood farther and farther apart when we threw the ball back and forth. I lobbed high balls high so he could learn to catch flies, and skimmed the ball across the grass so he could practice fielding grounders One day he came outside and told me there was something he wanted to learn. He wanted to catch a fly ball on the run. He came up with his own way to practice. He took a position in a corner of the yard, directed me where to throw, and raced to catch it. This would continue for years until the yard was just too small for it to be a challenge. As for the rules of baseball, he picked them up on his own by watching hours of Yankees' games on TV.

Knowing how to catch flies in your backyard, however, is not the same as knowing how to play baseball. Knowing how to play baseball means knowing how to play on a team in a real game So we signed him up for coach pitch baseball. Coach pitch baseball follows T-ball. It hadn't occurred to me that I should have signed him up for T-ball. In T-ball, the ball sits on a tee the height of a kid's swing. It can take several tries, but eventually, a swing connects, and even if the bat only just catches the top of the ball and the ball falls off the tee to roll a few inches from the plate, everyone cheers as the child runs to first base. In coach pitch, the child's own coach tosses the ball to him rather than an opposing pitcher. He throws it so the child can hit. This way, the child gets used to a ball coming at him. T-ball teaches a child a level swing at a stationary target positioned precisely where the bat and ball should connect. Coach pitch lets the child connect that level swing to a baseball in flight.

For parents, T-ball and coach pitch baseball games were almost like a picnic. Coaches and parents set up a little diamond in the grass. At one particular game, Rubin played third base. That day, I watched from that side of the field, very near the base, but mostly, I chatted with Chuck, the left fielder's father. Across the infield and the outfield we could see the usual array of attention spans. Some kids looked at their gloves, some took the "ready position" they'd been taught, while one or two of the outfielders picked dandelions. Suddenly, to everyone's surprise, a kid hit a pop fly. It sailed up the third base line right to Rubin, who stood as he had seen the third baseman stand on TV, near enough to the base to reach it, but far enough to field a ball hit between him and the shortstop.

What happened next is what I remember.

When the runner on third saw the ball sail into the air, he ran down the third base line toward home. It wasn't that the runner assumed no one would catch the ball. It was just that runners always ran when the ball was hit. Rubin caught the ball easily, stepped on the base, and then trotted off the field even before his teammates realized he had turned a double play to end the inning. On the way, he casually tossed the ball without looking to see where the pitcher stood.

Chuck said, "Wow, look at that."

"Look at what?" I said.

Chuck explained. There'd already been an out from the boy who'd been thrown out at first. The fly Rubin caught was the second out. Although the runner on third was allowed to leave the base, if Rubin stepped on the base before the runner got back, the runner was out. That was the third out. So, Rubin turned a double play to end the inning. I don't remember this moment for Rubin's skillfulness. I remember it for his casual confidence. In one smooth motion he caught the fly, turned, stepped on the base and started for the dugout, making sure to leave the ball behind.

Many different kinds of knowledge were enfolded into that motion, a year's worth of routine and practice so that once he saw the ball leave the bat, he would moved toward it, watch it, and position himself to catch it. Before the ball had been hit, he stood where he needed to stand, a position he learned from watching games and from his coach's instruction. He understood and could explain the rule that made the double play possible. He was aware of the runner to his right. At one point, to know the rule meant he could recall it and explain it to me if I asked while we watched a game on TV. But in the moment he caught the ball and put the runner out, "to know" meant to act, to understand, to be aware, to stand and to move. "To know" meant "to do," and "to do" meant to think with his body and senses. The process of learning and practice that broke down what he needed to know into parts that could be apprehended now cohered. Another kind of knowledge made itself apparent to Rubin. His coach could tell him about it, and gesture towards it, but Rubin would only get a full view as he practiced. Call it "intuitive knowledge" or "feel" or call it an "eye" or "awareness," but one thing is true: that knowledge happened in time and space, in a particular moment at a particular place. Rubin expressed his understanding of the game of baseball and the way to play third base by catching the ball and putting the runner out. Of course, then, to catch a fly and turn a double play was miraculous, an event. Now, twelve years later, to miss that fly or to catch it and not put the careless runner out would be a mistake.

2

Once, during the first or second year of my career as a college writing teacher, a student raised his hand in class and asked, "How did you do that?"

I don't remember exactly what I was doing at the time, but I believe I'd put some sentences on the board and showed the class how they could rewrite them to make them clearer. I remember the sensation I felt just after I made the sentence different and better with a few quick chalk strokes. It was joy. I was in my twenties, in front of one of my first college writing classes, doing work I believed was an essential good. Teaching writing, I believed, could transform a student's relationship to herself and the world, give her power, and even keep her safe. I was lost in a process that gave me great pleasure: rewriting. For a moment, I nearly forgot the students were there.

It's an excellent question, an elemental one for a good teacher: How did you do that? For my students, in that moment, I only answered the question, "What does it look like when you know how to do that?" Like the moment when my son caught a fly and put out a runner at third base, different kinds of knowledge were enfolded in that moment. A scant bit of direct instruction about grammar which I had developed through trial and error and reading into a few rules of thumb I could tell you only if I stopped for a moment to figure out what they were. I knew I could do it, rewrite something, which is not a belief that every writing student has when she comes into a classroom. It's common for students to behave as if they have a limited number of sentences they can make in a given context. I possessed what could be called "skilled perception." What a gardener sees in a garden is very different from what I see. It's safe to say that I see hardly anything at all. To me, a garden is a backdrop. If I begin with the evidence of my eyes, I can see that some blooms are crisp along the edges and others are beginning to uncurl from their stems. I can notice, if I take the time, where soil is wet and dry. I can see where weeds have choked a bed. If I want to follow this path of observation and consciously choose to, that path can eventually cross the path of the gardener who has spent seasons with the garden, who calls plants by name and knows when to plant them. I was like a gardener in a garden; my eye right away drifted to the places they should to see what would make a difference to the choices I might make.

In *Ethical Know-How*, the cognitive scientist Francisco Varela describes two cognitive states, *deliberation and reflection,* and *spontaneous action.* We rely on deliberation and reflection when we encounter an unfamiliar world. In time, when that world becomes familiar and comfortable, we act spontaneously. The student who asked, "How did you do that?" brought me to my senses, and now I had to use those senses if I was going to understand what I had done, or express what I had done, let alone teach what I appeared to know.

3

Sometimes I write on the blackboard:

Oregano
Can tomatoes
Garlic
Olive oil

I ask the class, "What is this?"
The students respond, "A grocery list."
Except for the one who cooks who says, "It's a recipe."
The others reply, "But you already have to know what to do."
They're right, of course. If you know what to do, a list can be a recipe. When you look at that list with everything you know, everything you know acts like a hidden commentary. After a certain point in any cook's education, some oregano, a can of tomatoes, a few cloves of garlic, and bottle of olive oil set on the table is already a sauce:

Heat a pot.
Add the amount of oil in the time it takes to say the words "olive oil."
As soon as the scent of garlic reaches you from the pan, add a can of whole tomatoes. Remember: open the can before you add the garlic. If you have to stop, the garlic will burn and turn bitter. You'll have to start again.
Add salt and pepper, dried basil, and oregano.
If the herbs are fresh, add them toward the end.
Simmer, sometimes two hours, sometimes half an hour, depending on dinner time.
Add salt and pepper.
That recipe was the first I ever learned. I had plenty of what educators call "intrinsic motivation" when I learned it. I'd invited someone I'd fallen in love with to dinner and asked Ed, my college roommate, if he had any ideas, and he told me to get a can of tomatoes, some garlic, some oregano and an onion, then chop the garlic and onion, sauté

them, add the tomatoes and simmer it. Add salt and pepper, too. Put it on pasta.

Ed gave me a can of tomatoes he had a bottle of olive oil. He also had a little jar of dried basil. At the co-op, I found one sad onion and a head of garlic. It was Friday and the wholesale run wasn't until Monday morning. I found bag of spinach pasta. Fancy.

The cooking went off without a hitch. It was, I think, the first time I could properly say I cooked something, even though I'd opened a recipe book every now and then on a special occasion at home. That Ed told me the recipe is important. I'd cooked enough that I knew what the dish would taste like when it was done and I knew what it would look like when I served it. By "cooked" I mean I paid attention at every step. I noticed the whole tomatoes in the can floating in juice. I smelled the garlic when it hit the hot pan. I kept an eye on the clock so I wouldn't overcook the pasta. I tasted the sauce to make sure it was good enough to serve.

Over the years, that sauce became a routine part of my everyday menu. It appears on the family table once a week or once every ten days, depending on the rotation: chili, rice and beans, pasta with sauce and cheese, salty roast chicken, something I-don't-know-what yet—order a pizza. When a dish calls for red sauce, I use a version of the one Ed taught me. I never buy sauce in a jar unless I know time is short, however, when I make it, I make twice as much so I have some to freeze. I learned that cumin makes it Mexican, curry powder makes it Indian, garlic and oregano make it Italian. Stock, vegetables, and beans make it soup.

After a certain point, I knew some things in the recipe were up to me. "Up to me" became the recipe. If I want it chunky and rustic, I'll serve it over pasta shaped like flowers, or ears, or wheels, or corkscrews. If I want something that suits spaghetti or pizza, I puree it or put it through a strainer. In a hurry, I mash it all up in the pan with a potato masher.

When I began to see people do other things, I thought, "I'll try it that way." I used to chop an onion and sauté it in the olive oil before I added garlic, but then I read in an interview that Marcella Hazan cuts an onion in half and lets it stew rather than chopping and sautéing it. This is wonderful; it leaves a pale husk to eat when the sauce is done.

Twenty years ago, I saw Francis Ford Coppola on a cooking show. He puts butter in his sauce. And then there's that scene in *The Godfather* when the family goes to the mattresses and Clemenza teaches Michael Corleone to make the sauce by adding sausages and meatballs to the pot after he fries the garlic but before he adds the tomatoes. If I saw it, I tried it. In time, I "thought with" the recipe; it became a way to understand what I could do with certain ingredients.

4

I watch the cooking channel.

Although I can't I'd like to walk my knuckles back like a restaurant chef when I slice vegetables. The cook- book I learned the most from was Edward Espe Brown's *Tassajara Cookbook*. Although I didn't adopt the cuisine, I adopted its sensibility and took advantage of the diagrams and instructions, which were presented simply in small paragraphs. A recipe contained steps and listed ingredients with rough amounts, or none at all. The book talked about techniques, precepts, and principles. What binds a casserole? When does soup become stew? One recipe in particular stood out for me, the recipe for salad dressing. Brown explains why the ratio of one part tart to three parts oil is a good starting point. He describes, as he often does, what and why certain ingredients can be substituted, but starts with what's most common. He explains very simply what ginger, garlic, mustard, and soy sauce do, so you know why to add one or another; he explains how vinegar can become lemon, or olive oil can substitute for peanut oil. Garlic adds body, and mustard adds bite.

The Tassajara Cookbook taught me how, when it comes to cooking as well as writing, the process is the product. I learned that an ingredient can be subject to many different techniques. Whether I steamed, sautéed, simmered, blanched or combined them depended on my mood, the occasion, and what was available to me. *The Tassajara Cookbook* offered a unique structure that enabled me to work comprehensibly at the edge of my competence. Eventually, with time and practice, I could imagine how raw ingredients cooked, and how, when certain ingredients combined, they made something taste Italian, Greek, or Chinese.

Another benchmark in my cooking life was when my relationship to cookbooks changed. Someone gave me Jacques Pepin's *La Technique*, essentially a book of pictures of hands. Several hundred pages long, it begins with sharpening a knife and chopping an onion, and continues on through deboning a chicken and making puff pastry. Each simply titled section consists of a sequence of pictures with captions, preceded by a brief introduction. The photographs tell one story, the captions tell another. I leaf through its pages to look at things I would never do, and things I haven't yet done and might, and things I want to do, and things I am doing right now. It's become a reference book, the way the *Fannie Farmer Cookbook* has, and the *Jewish Holiday Cookbook*, and the *Joy of Cooking*, but a particular kind of reference book, the kind I use when I know what I am looking for as well as when I don't. I check instructions to firm up my understanding of what I am about to do, or remind myself of proportions or ingredients.

People who teach writing assign handbooks and worry over getting their students to use them. New handbooks are meant to become standard, but they rarely become, as far as I can tell, cookbooks. When I open a cookbook, I find flour between pages sticky with brown sugar. The cookbook becomes part of the life of the kitchen, but the handbook rarely becomes part of the life of the student's workroom because writing rarely becomes part of a student's life. I can imagine cooking without a cookbook—I do it every day. But I can't imagine my kitchen without cookbooks because when I need them, they are indispensable to me. Unfortunately, students don't always know what they need.

5

In time, I developed rules of thumb.

Stock the pantry. Oil, salt, pepper, garlic and herbs and spices that accumulate around the dishes I make the most, and some things I might try again. Always try to have an onion, garlic, a can of tomatoes, stock, pasta, rice, and carrots on hand.

Don't suffer over failures. Tomorrow I'll have another dinner to make.

Anything served at dinnertime is dinner.

Taste as I go.

Don't walk away from something when it's on the burner, or at least not for long.

Don't put a grease fire out with water. Smother it with salt or a pot lid. That's not so much a rule of thumb as a rule.

Ideally, I clean as I go, but I know that even when I clean as I go, there will still be a mess at the end.

If it says to preheat, putting something in the oven sooner won't make it cook faster.

A watched pot will boil, but I should be doing other things while the water is coming to a boil.

There is a lot of time in a kitchen, but only if I do several things at once.

I can only do several things at once if I don't do them at the same time.

Eventually, I'll learn how to know when something is done.

6

I've accumulated tools.

Slotted spoons
Rubber spatulas
Tongs
A chef's knife
A bread knife
A paring knife
Three cutting boards
A colander
A strainer
A sauté pan
An omelet pan
A big pot for soup
A pot for pasta
A cast iron pan
Pans to braise and roast in
Cookie sheets
A big whisk and a small one
A grater
A microplane
A meat thermometer

7

Once I was in a housewares store looking over the wall full of peelers and egg separators. I was in my mid-twenties. Eavesdropping, I heard one woman tell another, "I've closed two kitchens." She went on to specify that the kitchens were her mother's and her aunt's. My father saved a few things from his mother's kitchen: a food mill, two pots, and a sharp knife. The knife had been sharpened so often that the edge curved a bit at the middle, a little "s" shape from handle to tip. The blade bent whenever I tried to cut with it, but my father can always make it work. Of the things my grandmother handled, these I think were the ones she handled most. They were quite meager in their way. I used the food mill until it broke. In a thousand years, these items might not be interesting even to an anthropologist; they'd be like oyster shells and antique bottles turning up at the site of nineteenth century outhouses. They will never be ancient, not even antique.

Tools find hands. They live hands that hold them.

8

I'm the person everyone says "There's nothing to eat!" to, which means there is nothing they want to eat or nothing in the fridge that doesn't need to be cooked. I practice every day. Challenges operate at different levels of scale. There is the mundane cycle of dinners: chili appears every eleven days, pasta with red sauce and mozzarella cheese every nine, breakfast for dinner in a pinch. The audience for these meals values reliability and familiarity. Then there are meals that call for planning and preparation. The audience for those meals appreciate the dramatic, like a cold soup or goose, or the reliably executed traditional, like a holiday brisket, or a clear golden chicken soup with matzo balls. The same tactics and timing that make it possible for me to cook dinner in a hurry enable me to put dinner for two dozen on the table at roughly the time I promise.

Like the academic writing I teach, the cooking I do can be menial and profound, an opportunity and a chore. I make hundreds of meals a year and shop for them. My kids eat what I serve or they don't. Sometimes the meals are excellent, sometimes perfunctory. Most of the time I'm pressed for time, and sometimes I serve breakfast for dinner. I'm not responsible for creating new dishes or innovating old ones. I'm not responsible for developing menus or maintaining consistency the way chefs must be in a restaurant kitchen. The kinds of bright ideas I have in the kitchen revolve around two considerations: what I guess someone might like, and what I see when I look into my refrigerator or scan in the grocery store. Then suddenly I may understand what I might make that night. I can see the dish in my mind and see how it is made. I can see what I might do with an ingredient and imagine the outcomes. No foams, no lemon essence flash frozen into pearls scattered across the plate, but maybe fried chicken and a lentil salad.

The moment I realized I knew what it might be like to "know how to cook" was when I made a midnight snack for someone. We were hungry and it was way past dinner time. There was nothing in the fridge and very little in the cupboard, so I boiled pasta, then dressed it with what I found in the pantry: soy sauce, sesame oil, peanut oil and mirin, a sweet rice wine used in Japanese cooking. When I dressed the hot pasta, the smell jumped back at me. We ate it right from the bowl I served it in, watching TV in bed.

I'd gone to the cupboard and seen all the parts as one thing. When I went to the kitchen, it was already there.

COMMENTARY: IMAGINE THE STORY YOU TOLD OF YOUR LIFE AS A WRITER AS A WIDE SEA

Imagine the story you told of your life as a writer as
A wide sea you'd cross island by island
A desert you'd cross well by well
Or a stairwell comprised of erratic landings,
Twelve steps from one to another,
Ten from that one to the next
All the way to the top.
Think of each island, well, each landing,
As a moment you gathered yourself,
And acted more skillfully than before.

Identify those moments. Describe them.
Begin anywhere.

Are their places ahead of you or above you?

Imagine them.

COMMENTARY: START WITH SOMETHING YOU DO

Start with something you do, whether you are good at it or not, but something you do, or have done consistently—something that required your attention, something you have tried to be good at. Perhaps something where it doesn't matter if you become an expert, or even particularly good.

Try something other than your work, other than writing, other than teaching, and other than your professional occupation.

****

Write the story of how you learned to do it.
Describe what you had to learn to do it.
Describe what it looks like when you are doing it well.
Describe what it looks like when you need to learn more.
What did you need to be told?
What did you learn for yourself?

Think of when you are doing your best work.
From outside, what would it look like?
From inside, what does it feel like?

Think of the classes you've created:.
When you are teaching well, what does it look like? From the outside?.
What does it feel like? From the inside?.
When the students are working well, how does it look?

Think of the people whose work you admire,
What do they need to know to do their best work?
What do they need to learn when they fail?

THIS ABILITY

1

For many years, every time I sat down to write, I asked myself "What does it mean to know how to write?"

It wasn't that I couldn't write at all. I could put words to paper. I could write a poem. I could even, in a modest way, write a song. And I could always talk. But the closer the lines got to the right hand margin, the more confused I became, and the less at home I felt in words. The problem grew as I went further in school—first into high school, then into college, where the means of making myself visible to the people who taught me was the academic paper.

I'd like to describe my "learning disability" to you.

I say "I'd like to" because I'm not sure I can, which I think is part of the experience, so it's worth lingering over the reasons why I hesitate here, at the moment when I intend to speak about it directly.

There are several reasons for my hesitation. My learning disability is invisible. It's not on or of my person. When you see it, you see its traces in memos, reports, and papers.

I wonder if you'll believe me, or if you will think I'm describing a person who, with persistence, resilience, practice, or the right writing teacher *would* learn "to write". Or that I'm describing a uniquely undisciplined person.

These suspicions—that I might not be telling the truth, that I might be exaggerating, that I might need to work harder, that I'm lazy, or lack gifts—well, I, too, have wondered.

I didn't know or understand myself to have a learning disability until I was twenty-two, almost thirty years ago, when my English professor, Bob Stein, suggested that one might be the source of the problem I had with writing. I was evaluated twice over the next five years, and both times a sympathetic professional said the same thing: what you experience is evident in how you test. They talked about higher order thinking and spatial memory. They summarized the narrative sections in the reports and explained the charts and graphs.

Yes, they said, you have what we would call a learning disability. If they gave me a name for it, I don't remember what it was, but a name wouldn't have made a difference. Testing divided my understanding of how I learned and how I wrote into two parts. In the first part, I thought I was unable to do something I desperately wanted to do. In the second part, the problem had a cause. But the word *cause* isn't quite right because it suggests that I could draw a line between my experience and the work I produced—*cause, effect*. The idea of a cause suggests that I could intervene strategically at some point and change the course of the effect. If you want a better night's rest, for example, drink less coffee and exercise more. Not true with a learning disability.

Before my experience was called a learning disability, it was only the way I moved in the world; afterward, I moved in a way with a name. More to the point—a learning disability is not something I have, it's something I do.

How do I do it?

Sometimes, it's like hitting a baseball and finding that I can only run counterclockwise. Instead of first base, I run to third.

Dropped words, missed letters, misread directions, getting lost on the way to places I've been twenty times.

Like dropping a box of nails on the floor, picking them up one at a time, and always leaving one to step on.

Typos. Tangled syntax.

Sentences go up like the stairs left in the wreck of a demolished house and stop; or they knot like a spooled-out kite string.

Paragraphs move incrementally forward without apprehensible transitions.

Sometimes my learning disability has the quality of a strange or very bad dream. A wall map where the rivers and roads slide off and leave the map blank. I try and catch them but my arms are full and I drop them. I have to sort through and put them back.

A thicket grows up around my ankles as I walk that I don't notice because my walking makes it grow.

One little decision leads to another little decision, and then I am someplace far from where I started and not much nearer to where I intended to go.

Once, for a graduate school class, I was asked to submit twenty pages and wrote about two hundred. Many of those pages said the same thing but in a different order, or the same thing with a very slight change that seemed crucial to me.

One night, desperate, I sat in the middle of my living room with all two hundred pages fanned around me. They may as well have been blank; it seemed they could go in any order at all.

Or take the time I drove from New York City back to Ithaca and it took nine rather than four hours. Not because of an accident or because I was pulled over or because the highway was being repaved all the way from the George Washington Bridge to the Delaware Water Gap. A slight change changed everything. I went downtown toward the Holland Tunnel instead of uptown to the George Washington Bridge. All went well as I drove down Sixth Avenue. Then, in quick traffic, I misread a sign, lost my nerve, and took the Lincoln Tunnel. Suddenly, nothing looked familiar. I drove along a river through a New Jersey landscape of small towns, one after the next, that mixed industrial parks, suburban housing, strip malls and churches from a hundred or two hundred years ago. Each time I stopped at a gas station for directions, I walked away knowing less than I did when I walked in. I crawled out of New Jersey in little hook-shaped advances that took me a few miles forward, then halfway back, and a little bit further in the opposite direction from where I'd been drifting.

Finally, I asked for directions back to the George Washington Bridge and began again.

Typically, I let other people do the driving. I can't, however, let other people do the writing.

2

To think of how I "do" my learning disability only in terms of what happens between me and a page, between a person and a process, or between brains, eyes, and ears ignores a defining dimension. Learning disabilities are experienced between individuals and institutions. Long before I was told I had a learning disability, it became one as soon as schoolwork demanded things I found myself unable to do—things classroom instruction didn't mitigate. I was ill-adapted to institutions' demands. While my learning disability made trouble between me and the page in private, it also made itself a disability in public, in the company of others and between me and teachers. School reinforced what and how to know. School schooled me. It tied learning to time, taught me how to use tools, where to sit and when to get up and move.

In school, my disability was like a dropped dish.

Never underestimate how angry a paper full of errors makes some teachers. Some treated me as if I'd used a leaf of the *New Testament* to roll a joint off a picture of their kids. It wasn't only disapproval at my apparent carelessness, but a real anger at what struck them as my disdain for their classes and with it the enterprise of teaching English. I don't think it's an exaggeration to say that some saw in my work a weakness in my character, a transgression against a commonly held virtue, like cleanliness, a good attitude, or promptness.

I don't blame them. Every draft I submitted looked like a first draft. They couldn't know that the draft was likely the fifth or seventh. At times, there was disbelief. One teacher simply said, "Listening to you, I thought you were smarter." Some were baffled. An exhausted college professor handed me the long required research paper I spent hours on and said, "I just don't know how to help you fix this. Maybe look at passive constructions?" I once turned in a paper early, proud and eager. A week later, the professor handed it back, stunned, like he'd come home early to a house he'd left his teenager watch for a week. The worst part was that the elevator didn't close quickly enough and I had to stand next to him for the ride down. Several weeks after I resubmitted it, he handed it back and said, "Don't you see the difference?" I could, but I didn't know how I'd done it. A friend helped.

It's impossible to separate how I feel from how I do my learning disability. We learn how to feel about who we are in the world, and school, like the family, is one place where even if you have evidence to the contrary, you believe the bad things that have been said about you. Over time, expectations became habits, and habits became predictions for which I seemed to have endless evidence. I developed an autonomic response to the act of writing that distorted my perceptions and limited my choices. When I am doing my learning disability and feeling as I did in the past, I'm like a toddler trying to pick up the stick she's standing on. I persist in the belief that if I try harder and work longer, a solution will appear. Human beings have an inexhaustible capacity for convincing themselves to do the opposite of what would work. I developed the habit of going over one paragraph again and again, tuning, fine tuning, revising, editing, moving things around; later, I developed the habit of producing endless, sprawling pages that in the end I couldn't make into something that someone else could read. Writing too little or too much became "how I wrote". How I wrote was who I was, like my tendency to wear my shoes out on the outer edge of the sole and heel. I've seen this with writers, learning disability or not, my whole career. People often see how they write as something like being left-handed. They produce what they are able to produce, which is a symptom of who they are.

Have I solved the problem of my "learning disability"? If solving the problem means "Did I make it go away?", I'd say no. But I work with its reality. As helpful as it was to understand my experience as one of *disability*—not *inability*, it doesn't come with an attendant cure. There are certain problems I've solved. For example, the computer makes it very easy for me to narrow the margins of a page and, for one reason or another, a four-inch margin is easier for me to read, edit, and proof than the standard one-inch margin. Text-to-speech software is miraculous, really. I've had to come to terms with the fact that anything I want someone else to read, I have to listen to. It's different from my own voice, which helps with poems; I never use text-to-speech for poems, except to proof. But in prose, listening to a piece helps me see where the links between parts or between sentences are broken or unresolved or unrealized or unmade.

Every writer who perceives himself as a writer with a problem imagines that everyone else writes more efficiently and easily. I have to remind myself continuously that this is bullshit and a dead end. This kind of thinking hinders the work. It isn't even the kind of tension, like doubt, that actually has a creative use. It's the specter of incapacity or inability.

When I began to step back and look at myself as someone who was not unable, but someone who was able in particular ways to accomplish what other people did, I began to work differently. When I am doing my learning disability and feeling as I did in the past, I persist in the belief that if I try harder and work longer, a solution will appear. I now understand that working over days, rather than hours, helps me see the work more clearly as it unfolds. To write consistently in small increments does me favors that grinding out long stretches didn't and couldn't. I can focus better without losing track of the whole.

Gradually—and by gradually I mean a little at a time over years—I saw that my goal shouldn't be to fix the way I worked or thought. I accepted the discontinuity in my thinking, and now I let myself put a single sentence on a page, then another, and then shuffle what I've collected. I make glue and scissors part of my work. I cut up drafts and reconstruct them, which helps me see how parts connect and make something new. I can cut all the empty words, the wind-ups and dead sentences, and put together what's left, which makes me more likely to write what I need to write and accept the sound of it. It's a process that helps me write when words alone won't.

I draw. Stepping back from the roar of words, or the tangle of them, whatever metaphor works at the time, has a salutatory effect on the outcome. Since I have a problem seeing a whole or seeing my way to a whole drawing lets me do that, frees me to work with symbols I can elaborate upon later so I don't get bogged down in a thwarted effort to express myself. I accept that I need to craft expression in a certain way if I am ever going to arrive at a point. Non-native speakers and novice writers need to accept this, too. More drafts are part of the solution, but drafts with goals: only to untangle sentences, only to edit, only to proof.

I separate form and content. Form is triggering, and sometimes it's just enough of something to get me through to the next thing. People who work with students with learning disabilities, and often students themselves, ask me how to help with organization. Associative organization, incrementally moving away from what I intend to say, can lead me into problems that in the past I had no perch from which to observe. To people who ask me about "organization" I usually say, "It depends." Do you want to help them learn what to do right now? Is time short? Then I might offer something that structures work from the outside, like classical argument structure with its opening and summary and proofs and acknowledgement and response. There are several effective ways, too, to help people structure an argument before organizing a paper. For example, concept maps, which link elements not just with lines but with words that relate various parts of the map to one another.

But these are techniques and tools and stopgaps, things any novice or experienced writer might do to get control of the product or the process. In general, though, my relationship to the whole enterprise of writing has had to change. Writing was hard, painful, and frustrating. I felt shame and anger along with the conviction that my capacity to write was fundamentally damaged. No strategy I know would make a difference if I didn't change that relationship. And nothing may be harder than choosing self-acceptance over shame. Jetsunma Tenzin Palmo, in her book *Into the Heart of Life*, calls an attachment to the beliefs I had about my worth or ability as a writer the "laziness of feeling unworthy." When I read that description, it hit me like new love. It was true. I saw every failure, false start, and draft I couldn't mend or any project I'd abandoned as evidence of a fundamental inability to write. This was more than the mild self-reproach I felt when, halfway to work, I remembered that folder I left on the kitchen table. These beliefs still root me to the spot when I'm at the threshold of some discovery or some opening-up. Called "laziness," these feelings become obstructions, an unclear view, an unskillful way to work with my learning disability. None of what I've learned about how to help myself and others write would matter if I hadn't become free enough to think of myself as someone who could orchestrate a complex process.

3

Now when I think of my learning disability, I think of my daughter's bedroom. She's a neatener, so it's not the mess I'm thinking of. It's that nothing ever leaves the room, and everything in it has a use. That little Playmobil baby and its car seat, all the teeny tiny plastic cups and plates that always appear when the game calls for them. It doesn't matter if they are jumbled with trees and waterfalls and plastic wagon wheels she'd put away haphazardly in the first place.

I think of the way she plays with them, these little houses with all their tiny cups and saucers and little spoons and bowls. Playmobil makes its people uniform in shape and size, although their races and outfits change. Line up the figures next to each other from several sets: Knight, Northern Explorer, Father at the Beach, Father at the Barbecue, and you can't help but meditate on the transmigration of tiny toy souls. But it's not knights-and- explorers she's playing, it's *family*. Dinners get cooked, kids go to school and fight with the friend who lives next door. So if she has a kid from a set in shorts, and a kid in a set with a bathing suit, she just switches kids when it's time to go to the pool. And if the hair color or style is wrong, she'll take the hair off the first one and put it on the other one—same kid.

When I think about my learning disability, I try to remind myself of how her game stretches across her room and across the apartment. I find clutches of people on the edge of the tub because it's a day at the pool, or under a chair because they're visiting the city. They all need to go someplace. Her room will have three homes set up as well as a school, each at a distance from each other so that leaving one place for another is a genuine *going*. When she doesn't have a house, or something else she needs, and there's no cash to buy it, she simply presses something else into service. She'll appear in the kitchen doorway to ask, "I need a pool with a slide. What would make a good pool with a slide?" And I'll look around the kitchen and ponder, and think about her toys, and offer ideas she'll accept and reject one after the next until she finds the right one. Most often, she'll make it herself, and when I see it, I'll know exactly what it is. There will be no mistaking it for anything but a pool with a slide even if the materials are unlikely and its shape a bit abstract.

I hope she'll hold on to this courage, this feeling that it is nobody's business but hers what she makes or what it looks like. Once, I found wet cat litter on the edge of the tub, and rice, too, scattered in the tub and on the floor. She'd been trying materials for beach sand. This was one time I said, "In the future, you'll have to use your mind for that."

I remember when it was all horses, maybe when she was six or seven. She had none to pretend with, so she made one. She took a stool and wrapped electric tape around the end of each leg. Then she found a forgotten unicorn costume to drape over it, leaving just the head exposed. Over the body of the costume she laid a towel, and over that a blanket for a saddle. She tied three of my ties together and made loops at each end to make stirrups. She found a bit of rope for reins. Then she'd rock back and forth to ride the "horse." She felt no need to show it to anyone. I walked into the room with the pocket doors and found the stable where she had a bucket full of oatmeal for feeding, and straw I used to cover the garden beds on the floor. There it was, by the trough.

Who would get angry at such a thing, such a work? I fell into saying things like, "Make sure you clean the stable." Good work draws the people around it into its reality.

I hear her through the door going through the voices and narration of the game she's playing with her tiny people and houses, or I see her go past the kitchen doorway. (Somehow, I'm almost always in the kitchen.) I've heard a loud "Papa" so often that I call, "Is that me or in the game?" before I stop what I'm doing to see what she wants.

If I enter the room when a game is in progress, it stops until I leave. Good girl. The privacy you need to do this thing is a part of the process. I leave her be until absolutely necessary. Like "Never wake a sleeping baby," so, too, "Never interrupt a child deep in a game" is an axiom parents know without being told.

We've developed a routine. If I'm simply entering to leave a sock or a book, I act like nothing is going on, and she doesn't stop, embarrassed, until I leave. But the first time I found her lying on the floor near one of the houses all set up, quiet, staring at the ceiling I had to ask if everything was okay.

She interrupted her trance halfway to say, "I'm just doing the part of the game in my head that I can't do with the things I have."

When I think of my learning disability, I would like to remember the casual sense of entitlement my daughter feels that lets her solve problems about how to make the game work rather than abandoning it because a solution isn't apparent at the outset. And I think of how I come into the room to find a clear floor after days when it was populated by families in their backyards and on trips to school. All the travels to the tub/beach, all the nights when she took ten minutes to put the 'kids' to bed, each in their own rooms and under covers, a ritual that had to be finished before she could get into bed, all swept up. I still ask with spontaneous concern, as if it has never happened before, "What happened? You didn't need to clean up the game" and she says matter-of-factly, "It was finished."

I can tell how deeply this is hers, because she can let go so lightly.

My journey through being schooled in writing has been a kind of folktale in which I set out as a young man to some place I could see across a valley from my roof, only to arrive at it middle-aged. In such a story, along the way, the hero encounters trials and teachers. He might win his name, he might win self-knowledge, and he might win the princess or the kingdom. What I won was this book.

When I think of how I work with my learning disability now, I think of a box of broken crayons. All the colors I need. No, all the colors I can use. No, all the colors available to me. No, my colors. The colors I have. So it's not a box of fifty-two, or a hundred and four, or two hundred and eight, with a cool sharpener built into the box. It's a box of eight. Eight fat crayons.

I'm drawing a plan for this piece—lines radiating from a box of broken crayons in the middle of the page. Lines I have thinkened (thickened, really, but that's the kind of mistake that is the learning disability's gift to me) to connect the box of broken crayons with seven words: *Process teaching perspective emotion learning attraction doubt*. And more thickened lines that radiate from them. I make more lines.

Mark the painter sits next to me at the café where I write. He sees my picture making and asks me if I like the way the marker felt on the paper. "I see you bought Prismacolor markers. Brush tips."

I think, "Yes, yes, absolutely, markers or crayons, I just like the feeling of filling it in."

"That's what I tell my students," he said, "You know you're making something when you just like the feel of the paint against the brush and the paint on the canvas. You love the process for its own sake."

It's true. I fill in each box carefully and it's a beautiful thing. My mind settles. It feels very important and crucial. I can sneak around my words.

Another day the lady next to me says, "Those are Waldorf crayons."

"Oh yeah? Well, the colors are really bright. And they feel good to color with."

I used "color" out loud as a verb to describe what I was doing to another adult.

One thing my learning disability taught me: Who cares?

"You know what they're real good for?" she goes on, "Blending."

I know she's a teacher. A good teacher invites the stranger in and honors the oddball who loves his work.

"I never tried that." She's right.

Materials. The feel of things.

Words are material. They feel intractable to me, like the tunnel entrance is blocked and I'm digging out with my bare hands.

I took these crayons from my daughter, who finished with them a while ago and hardly misses them, although when she sees me with them, she reminds me she might need them sometime.

Good, I remember thinking. Your tools matter to you. Never give them away lightly, as if they belonged to no one.

I had to learn this.

4

I am thinking about G., a boy I know who has been told that he has a learning disability. His mother told me it cheered him up when his father told him that Einstein had a learning disability. I wonder if he felt relief.

I felt relief when Bob Stein suggested that a learning disability might be the cause of all my trouble when I wrote papers for school. I was much older than G., who is at the very beginning of his life as a reader and writer. I was twenty-two, and that was thirty years ago. Then, every time I sat down to write, I asked myself what it meant to know how to write. Even though I was older than G., I liked hearing stories about great people who had learning problems, too. But sometimes the encouragement I felt was tempered by another thought. When I heard that Einstein, or the scientist Michael Faraday, or the physicist James Clerk Maxwell had learning problems, I think, Sure, but I'm no Einstein, Faraday, or Clerk Maxwell.

Thomas West argues in his book *In the Mind's Eye: Visual Thinkers, Gifted People With Dyslexia and Other Learning Difficulties, Computer Images and the Ironies of Creativity* that what we call a disability, viewed in another way, reveals crucial gifts that a narrow view of disability as deficit ignores. West argues that Einstein's, Faraday's, or Clerk Maxwell's dyslexia, as a feature of their minds, also gave them cognitive advantages crucial to their work, advantages as evident as the interference dyslexia causes. My inability to perceive my differences as gifts stood in my way. By the time I learned to think of my struggles not as "inability" but "disability," the effects of that inability were woven into me like fibers into a rope. For me just to write some little thing, paper would be spread out everywhere, as if a giant paper snake had shed its skin. Putting my thoughts in coherent order on paper for an audience seemed like one long pratfall. Now, I see the advantage my gift for getting lost gives me, but that insight is new to me. G.'s parents already know his gifts. G's mother tells me of his intricate drawings of battles and machines, how he listens to stories while he makes things out of Legos. I imagine he sees as he goes, one thing after the next, and if one thing doesn't work, another will until he is sure; and if he is not sure, then he does it differently. No one taught him how to do this. He's lucky that this comes to him without effort, unlike some of the things school asks of him. My best wish for G. is that he knows that it is always within his grasp to be the happy genius of his own life. What I would say to G., except that it would only sound like blah blah blah to a boy his age, is that there are people waiting for his gift. Those people are already out there waiting to receive it, the way we wait for apples up at Littletree Orchard every year, because apple trees make apples, and there are so many kinds, and we love apples. And G. will make what he makes, and we will be waiting to receive it.

COMMENTARY: GIFTS

One thing that watching my own children go through elementary school changed for me is my understanding of what a "gift" is. I think I may have already believed this in some way. But as I watched my children age, and my children's friends and classmates go from grade to grade, I was struck by something that was quite humbling: school often defines gifts narrowly, to the extent that some young people don't know how important their gifts are. It was my children's teachers who taught me this. My children went to a very special public school. It wasn't special because it had a unique focus or did something particularly innovative. In every way it was like any public school in a small city, apart from the fact that its teachers *attended* to each child as a whole, evolving creature, and within the demands of reading, writing, arithmetic, and classroom management, made room for each child's gift. I began to look at my own students differently, and I thought about the people I'd known, and my own time in high school and how it contrasted with my brother and sister's experiences. There were the outstanding students, artists, and athletes, yes, but I also began to see there were people with many other gifts that now were quite obvious to me. One had a gift for creating connections between people; another was particularly good at making complicated tasks and ideas comprehensible; another, with very few items, could turn a shabby room into a space with its own peculiar beauty and comfort.

Please don't get me wrong. I want to avoid the notion that the one who makes connections between people should be a therapist, or the one who could make complicated things simple should be a teacher, or that the one who could transform a room should be an interior decorator. Our gifts manifest themselves in many contexts.

It is true that some people have a gift for chaos or for creating certain kinds of problems wherever they go. But I often think that's because another of their gifts has been thwarted in some way, or they find themselves in contexts unsuitable to them, or because something has intervened between them and their gifts. Whatever that thing is keeps them from knowing their own worth.

****

Spend a couple of days observing the people around you and see how many gifts you can identify. Creating some strangeness can help. Think of yourself as a zoologist whose great pleasure it is to wait for a butterfly they've never seen before to land, or a botanist in search of an orchid that people have known only by rumor.

Then ask, "What are my gifts, and where are they?" By "where" I don't necessarily mean "Why aren't they evident?" (although that may be a legitimate question) but where can I find them?

COMMENTARY: THE LISTENER

In writing classes, we talk a lot about "audience." We know that people write better when they understand their audiences, and students write better when they understand the purpose of their writing in terms of the goals they have for that audience.

But the only thing lately that helps me begin, especially when it's prose I'm writing, which is hard for me, is not to think about the audience but to think about *the listener*. The listener is the person I can speak quietly to. Wherever the work goes, I begin with an idea of who would simply sit across from me and listen.

****

It may be one person, or different people at different times, or an *idea* of who listens. Think of a listener. Who listens?

COMMENTARY: HOW DO YOU KNOW YOU ARE DONE

For many reasons, I've never felt about academic writing the way I feel about writing a poem. The most important reason is probably very simple: academic writing really isn't my "instrument." I'll struggle as much on a poem as I have on anything I've tried to write for journal in my field, but the quality of struggle is different. Academic writing has an unpleasant taste. Even when I despair at ever finding my way, when I work on a poem, in my heart's heart, I know without saying that I will find my way. I know I can find the choices to make and make them. That's never the case when I'm writing something requiring citations and a bibliography. I've thought hard about the differences, and in the end have concluded that they all come down to one thing. When I write a poem, I can tell for myself when I am done. I may share it, I may seek feedback, I may tinker over time, I may make a belated discovery that leads me to dismantle the whole thing, but I have a solid sense of when it's arrived at a point where it's finished. With academic writing, I never know when I am done.

****

Look back at the story of your work. How has your work changed? When has it changed? When has it stopped changing? Explore those moments when you knew you'd become better at what you do, when you acquired new skills or new confidence. Consider what contributed to those changes and how—and even when—you knew those changes were the right ones.

COMMENTARY: NAME YOUR MATERIALS, NAME YOUR TOOLS

Name your materials.

Name your tools.

How do you begin?

How do you know you are done?

Describe the pleasure you take in your work.

Describe the pleasure you take in something that you do, but don't do well.

How do you celebrate your success?

Think about a setback or disappointment in your work. Consider whether it led you to something you needed to learn and how it happened.

Celebrate that setback or disappointment.

FOUR THINGS

If, say, everything I spent the semester teaching left a student's memory but for four things, what would I want those things to be?

When you receive a new assignment, ask, "Have I seen something like this before?"

Before you start, ask, "How can I find out what I need to know?"

While you write, ask, "How far have I come? How far do I have to go?"

Before you give it away, ask, "Have I said this the way I meant to say it?"

A USER'S MANUAL

IDLING AT AN INTERSECTION

Idling at an intersection, I watched two men.
The slab of sidewalk at the corner dug up. Gravel poured.
Over the gravel, an iron net and rebar.
A form ready for concrete in the shape of a corner and curb.
The older man pointed to spots I could see would be trouble,
Where the ground dipped with the hill.
He swept the flat of his hand across the plane
Of concrete only they could see.
The young man stepped over the form.
He pointed out spots he thought would be trouble.
The older man nodded.
I come back to a smooth slab of concrete
That forgets the work that made it.

SOMETHING FROM NOTHING: THE WRITING TEACHER'S WORK

I want to talk to you about my work, a writing teacher's work.
But, for the time it takes to read this
I want to close the door on curriculum,
The common syllabus,
Outcomes and assessment,
Strategies for effective peer review,
Grading policies, and the calendar,
And evoke instead something else,
The something and the nothing
Out of which learning in the writing classroom takes place,
An else that often feels like making sculpture from smoke.
To evoke this thing I rely on an old medium,
The voice in your head.
If you are reading this you've lent it to me,
As students lend me the voices in their heads.
Thank you. I will assume with you, as I do with them,
The storyteller's imperative to bring news from far away,
A far away that is quite close,
And as mysterious as a house cat to Christopher Smart
And as familiar as a tiger to William Blake.
Of course, if I set aside the calendar
And which readings,
And which themes,
And how to assess,
And our syllabuses,
What is left?
This is the "Nick the Chopper" Question.
In *The Wizard of Oz*
The Wicked Witch of the East cursed Nick
To keep him from his beloved, Nimmee Aimmee.
She cursed his axe so it chopped off his limbs as he worked;
Ku-Klip replaced them, one at a time, even his head

Until, Voila—
Nick the Chopper became The Tin Woodsman.
As an aside, Ku-Klip kept Nick's "meat head" in a cabinet.
Nick's head insists that he,
Not the Tin Woodsman,
Is Nick the Chopper.
Do you get where I'm going with this?
Chop chop chop.
I set aside syllabus.
Chop chop chop.
I set aside the assignment sheet.
Chop.
I set aside the problem of citation.
Chop chop.
Etcetera etcetera.
Chop chop chop.
What of writing class is left?
A little bit of nothing?
A little bit of something?
What I would say is left is the *real work*.

Gary Snyder uses the phrase, "the real work"
To describe some of what I mean.
He uses the phrase here and there—in poems and essays.
An interviewer asked him
"What is the real work?" Snyder answers,
I think it's important, first of all because it's good to work— I love work;
Work and play are one. And that all of us will come back again
To the hoe in the ground, or gather wild potato bulbs with digging sticks,
Or hand-adze a beam, or skin a pole, or scrape a hive—
We're never going to get away from that…
He continues,
We've been living a dream that we're going to get away from that…
Work is always going to be there. It might be stapling papers,

It might be typing in the office. But we're never going to get away from that work,
On one level or another. So that's real. The real work is what we really do.
And what our lives are. And if we can live the work we do know that we are real,
And it's real, and that the world is real, then it becomes right.
And that's the work: to make the world as real as it is, and to find ourselves as real as we are within it.

What is the *real work* of the writing classroom?

Teachers must transmit what our students need to know,
Yet what we transmit is hardly even the half of it.
There is another knowledge which we also address in our plans and
  intentions:
Stuff you can only learn through experience,
Stuff that is manifest to others and apparent to ourselves
Only through the act of making something
And so the real work of teaching writers involves a fundamental
  tension
Between what we must tell students and what they can only know for
  themselves.

Let me put it another way:
My son made his first roast chicken recently
According to the recipe I told him,
The one he's watched me make for years.
He called to ask me,
How will I know when it's done?
And I had to think for a moment.
I have cooked a thousand chickens.
How do I know when it's done?
When it smells done.
When the time has passed that I know it is done.
And finally, when you prick the thickest part of the thigh with a fork
And the juice runs clear.
And he, who had never done it on his own before
Asks, *What is clear?*

71

We transmit the traditions, the tools, and forms we value,
But we also know that such knowledge hardly describes
What it means when we describe what and how a writer knows.
To know how, as the philosopher Gilbert Ryle puts it,
Is not to check first then act, but to act spontaneously,
Not to ask how and what first, then act,
But to be deeply imbued by what it is to act.
This does not mean we do not critique or reflect,
Especially when we are learning something new,
But that even those moments of "deliberation and reflection"
Move toward "spontaneous action" (as Francisco Varela writes)
When we are able to forget ourselves into the work we do,
Which allows us to create something right for each unique time and
    place.

So, the writing teacher creates a place,
Out of the clock and the calendar,
Out of the once and the now
Out of the assertion and the reason why.
We draw a circle around rooms full of writers,
We invite to work.
"Work" is a peculiar word for these peculiar classes we teach,
Though whenever I think about the writing teacher's art,
I begin and end with thoughts on our work.
"Work" stands for the product.
And "work" stands for the "process"
But in the writing classroom,
The process is the product,
And so it—the process—is a kind of artifact, too.

Work also refers to "the work."
When I am in a classroom,
By the third or fourth week,
If I have done my job well.
"the work" emerges.
It emerges in a way that is not mysterious but elemental,
Each student sets down "my work"—
By "my work" I mean the personal struggle—

And glimpses the common struggle.
We, the two of us or the ten of us, or the twenty-five of us,
Turn toward it, and regard it
As if we'd driven over a rise
To find our city pooled in mist
And the mist dissolves as we approach
And first we regard it at a distance
And then as we approach, it may disappear
And then it is all around us.

Each class is an invitation to inhabit
Forms of attention and attunement,
Patterns of caution and regard,
Machines of consideration,
Rhythms of what's done.
If all goes well, it is no more mysterious than
The heart and mind, that tangle we are always entangled in,
The heart and mind, for which there is no word that doesn't,
    inadvertently,
Evoke separation: the heartmind, which we hesitate to name *knowledge*,
But is knowledge—
My materials are words and forms and time and attention.
I shape experience, enter conversation strategically and spontaneously,
And direct a periodic return to some elemental act or event,
(the adze, the axe, the digging stick)
That repeats and elaborates upon itself.
The classrooms pile up behind me like the lifetime of beds I've slept
    in,
But I draw a circle around each one, and
Rather like my grandmother,
Who could make any kitchen her own
Simply by drawing a circle around it with her work,
Hand around the sharp knife, hand at the cutting board.
I invite my students to do the same as I do,
Hand at the keyboard, hand around the pen,
Screen and paper, the stapler,
Through which the work makes

The world clear and real and apparent,
A circle they can draw anywhere
At any time simply by taking up the work
As long as the work persists.

And so I enter every odd classroom,
Like the tailor in the Yiddish folk song,
Who seems to make a something from a nothing
That is never really a nothing.
First, he sewed his newborn daughter a blanket,
And when the blanket became worn and frayed at the edges,
And he saw her leaving it here and there,
He trimmed it and sewed it again,
And made her a little vest to wear,
And soon, she grew too big for it,
As she was bound to,
So, he cut it a bit and hemmed it,
And made her a scarf,
Which, when it became too short to keep out the cold,
He trimmed and stitched
Into a handkerchief for her.
When it, too, became worn and threadbare,
He made it into buttons,
A row for a pretty school dress.
And when the buttons were lost, one by one,
And there was no fabric left
To make something from a button
That was once a scarf,
That was once a vest,
That was once a blanket and
He made this story which I learned,
And which I have now told you.

THE KITCHEN CLASSROOM

The kitchens I learned in taught me how to get work done. Properly speaking, my grandmother's was the first kitchen that taught me. I remember her standing in her housedress all day, standing by the sink, peeling, slicing, and chopping. She'd slice a carrot by pulling a paring knife toward her thumb. Like classrooms, kitchens are simply rooms until the cook shows up and the eaters arrive. I come from a family of renters and apartment dwellers. Apartment dwellers occupy spaces that forget them, spaces meant to forget them. My grandmother, like many cooks, drew a circle around that room from the other kitchens it had been and would be. Her meals were part of the background; always there, I'd discover her work the same way I thought I discovered jazz in college.

I entered other people's kitchens and learned in them. I was made welcome in them. Ellen made meals in a day care kitchen, meals that were more interesting than the meals most kids ate home. She made simple meals with care and attention to flavor and texture that showed a love for the small hands that would eat them. The quiet that descends on a group of toddlers enjoying rice and baked chicken legs has a deep, mystical quality. Before I met Ellen, I can't say I understood flavor at all. Once, we both saw the same recipe in the *New York Times* magazine in 1991 for black beans by Rubin Blades. Each week we checked the back pages for the recipes. I made the recipe and she made the recipe. But she had a way of understanding what the recipe taught about the food, how the combination of ingredients worked together to transform each one into a new whole. She took cooking classes, but it struck me then that she was going to find something out, the way a book lover or autodidact might go to the library to figure something out, rather than be trained. She spoke in a whispery way, and since I was taller than she was, though not by much, she looked up when she spoke, behind glasses that made her eyes big, so when she talked about a new recipe, it was with reverence. She showed me how to read recipes for what was essential to learn in them, things that provided leverage for other meals and dishes later on—what made something Cuban, what made something Thai, the techniques that would make me more flexible and adaptable, capable of looking at the contents of my refrigerator and being able to see what was in it as dinner. From her, I learned how cooking for others is an act of communication, expression, reassurance, discovery, and comfort, all of which are layered into labor over mundane details of preparation, skill and technique.

The mother of my childhood friend Neil cooked out of *Gourmet* magazine. Mrs. Chase's meals stunned me. They were the first taste I had of food made with an attention to detail, to ingredients, and to methods and blends of spices and flavors. I remember a grilled sirloin I ate there. She chose a whole-grain mustard to go with it. The first broccoli I ever ate, I ate at her table. It also the first vegetable I'd ever eaten that hadn't been boiled, thawed, or rehydrated.

And then there is my mother, who did most of the cooking for our family, and found a way to do it, although she never liked it, and it showed. She persisted though, and found a way to feed u The old Betty Crocker recipe box, filled with recipe cards sent to her weekly as part of a "club" attest to her attempt to get better. Like her, I shop and make the everyday meals, executed when I get home from work. She hated to cook, and that seems fair. She was required to undertake a chore she had no feel for or love of, while I chose to take on something that interested me at first, then became a household chore.

In food terms, I grew up in a literacy-rich environment.

COMMENTARY: THINK OF YOUR CLASSROOM AS A POINT THAT A LINE PASSES THROUGH

Think of your classroom as a point that a line passes through. Think of the line as the work you teach your students to do. What is that work and how will it carry forward into the future?

AN IMAGE OF EXPERTISE

Although as teachers we tend to think more about the kind of writing our students will do, the kind of books they need to read, and the particular problems they need to solve, we begin with an image of expertise. We have a particular kind of person in mind who deals with writing in a certain way. Rather than describe what the writer I have in mind will write, I want to describe how she'll behave.

She seeks feedback, or at least information, including models or examples.

She makes the best of different kinds of feedback because she's going to get all kinds, and one kind may be silence.
I would be happy for her if she was able to tell whose feedback mattered.

She can talk about her work and process it in ways that may be idiosyncratic, but are concrete and particular.

She has a way of going about things. She can incorporate new information into her way, or can adapt her way when her ambitions change, or when she finds the way in its present form inadequate

She addresses the relationship between herself, her audience, the thing she's writing, and what's appropriate or possible for the time and place.

She can talk about aspects of a text that catch her eye or hold her attention along with what she considers effective, skillful or elegant, although she doesn't have to discourse on it like a critic, linguist, or grammarian.

She reads and observes like someone who makes things for herself.

She allows what she discovers along the way to put pressure on the product she imagines at the outset. She lets that evolving image guide her. When she works, she adapts.

She attends to what others take for granted.

She can, as Sara Ruddick writes in *Maternal Thinking*, "judge which questions are sensible, which answers are appropriate to them, and which criteria distinguish better and worse answers."

She can figure out what to ignore and what to look or listen for.

She makes thoughtful acquaintance with examples, models, and experiences.

She expresses her judgment through what she writes and through her decisions. If asked, she can explain her choices, although what she understands is expressed in her work.

She sees the difference between effective and ineffective language, the common and the unique, the conventional and the unprecedented.

She does these things when she has to.

She knows when she has to.

She believes she has to.

When she receives a new assignment or goes to a new place, she stops to ask herself: "Have I seen something like this before?" and "What do they want exactly?" and "What will I need to know do this?" and "Are they serious?"

COMMENTARY: THAT JUST SOUNDS LIKE WRITIING

A student once came to my office with something on her mind; it was the essay she was writing. She didn't understand the assignment. She had a problem, she said. Then she went on to talk about another essay she had read that was similar in some ways but very different from hers, really, when she thought about the voice and the subject. She described her idea, and then described the way the two parts of the essay would correspond with one another. Then finally she landed on the biggest problem, the conclusion. She couldn't write conclusions, she said, and that was her problem. Of course, she didn't have a problem, at least not in the way she thought. She wasn't inadequate to the task of writing. She didn't have a problem of understanding. "That's not a problem," I said. "That just sounds like writing." I explained how the way she talked about the problem was the way writers talk about it—some pieces are easy, some are hard. What she needed to learn, though, was that if she kept at it, she would solve that problem and move on to another one. But she would need to keep at it. She'd need to tolerate the open-endedness of some beginnings.

****

Create an image of expertise, but rather than describe what someone needs to know to do the work well, describe what that person needs to do. What kind of situations does she find herself in? How does she behave when she encounters those situations? What kinds of problems will she have to solve? When she needs to learn something new, what does she do? What do you do?

THE EMPTY ROOM

A writing class starts with an empty room.

An empty classroom is empty in a special way—like a Greyhound waiting room at 1:00 AM, or the empty streets on Christmas Eve in almost any city in the United States.

An empty classroom becomes an empty writing classroom when it's been assigned to a writing class.

I've found some version of the same thing in every classroom: a light switch, a blackboard (now, a whiteboard), desks attached to chairs and sometimes chairs with tables between them. Fluorescent light, landlord white, grey floor tiles. Some have the cast of despair familiar to anyone who has waited in the DMV; the best are clean, bright, and cleaned regularly. Some show the beating hundreds of students passing through lay on a room. Usually no tables, just desks with chairs attached, that species of combo desk and chair that sometimes comes with a basket underneath. These rooms have piled up behind me now like the beds I've slept in, teetering in a tower, crib on the bottom and a succession of single and queen-sized beds stacked on top, an inverted ziggurat, or rather like that leopard skin pill box hat Bob Dylan said balanced on Edie Sedgewick's head like a mattress on a bottle of wine. Lately, I've settled into the clean bright rooms of a well-supported public university, where the complaints I hear often have to do with whether the tables fit right or it's wired so that teachers and students can show their PowerPoint presentations. Still, each is fundamentally like the many non-descript rooms I've passed my life in, distinguished largely by what would happen to me the longer I stayed in them—another form to fill in, a test to take, a tooth to be drilled.

When I taught outside of universities, in community-based programs, the rooms varied more than those I encountered in colleges, save for the ubiquitous combo desk and chair. I taught in a small room meant for office space, in corners of a floor-sized open space, in a converted office among a suite of offices, and in windowless basement rooms probably meant for storage. The best room I taught in was in a former convent, a nice square room with desks and chairs arranged in a U with a row or two on the inside, long bulletin boards and blackboards. Classrooms now want more as there is more to want: smart boards, tools for multi-media texts, computer access for everyone. But that's the old wish: a place to write, something to write with, something to write on, and time.

The question is, how will the work we do together define the space we share?

COMMENTARY: ALL I KEPT THINKING

I heard an expression once, "The long way draws sweat; the short way draws blood." Once, on a snowy day, I saw that I could walk up a hill to the parking lot I needed to get to or I could take the long path around the apartments, which took me away, then back up another path. I took the short way. Midway through, I was standing calf deep in snow, panting, thinking that it would be okay if I just rolled back down, but I pressed on nonetheless. When I reached the top, there was a young man waiting. He said, "I watched you, and all I kept thinking was *Why didn't he just take the path?*

****

Sometimes there is a short way to learning something, a way that's worth taking. But there are many long ways that you have no choice but to take. Identify some short ways in how you learned your work and their consequences. Do the same for the long ways.

THE DINING ROOM CLASSROOM

I taught some writing classes for an adult education program at an expensive private college. The director of the program decided to solicit an alumni donation because she had a plan. She wanted a seminar table for the small room at the back of the building that housed the program office. The room already had desks with chairs attached, usually grouped in a circle, or in clumps where students worked in groups.

She wanted a table that a class could sit around comfortably, so she brought in some people from facilities to design and build it.

One day I came into class to find that new table. It was was oblong and filled the whole room, so that people would need to say "excuse me, pardon me" as they snuck between the wall and chair backs. Students could either spread out from one another around the perimeter, sit in a straight line along one side, or group together at one end, but the table was so big that it felt like the last table in that scene from *Citizen Kane* where Kane and his wife's growing alienation is illustrated by a succession of bigger and bigger dining tables.

This table caused much surreptitious eye rolling, and eventually facilities came back and removed a few feet from the center. The awkward shape it left behind still made the table feel like a plan to keep people apart, not to draw them together in the same space, as the director intended with good will and even a touch of joy: a seminar table.

In the humanities, the seminar is the gold standard for discourse and inquiry, the place where knowledge gets made and mastered. This seminar table left us further apart from one another than before, even though we were all sitting at the same table.

COMMENTARY: THE HOST MUST ALWAYS CHOOSE THE GOAT

Since much of what a writing student needs to learn only becomes apparent in the work they do, the successful teaching of writing depends a great deal on teachers learning as many ways to say the same thing as we can. It's important to remember that a metaphor has limits and can get in the way of thinking about something as well as helping you think about it. For example, writing can be like cooking, but the ingredients don't present themselves like the ingredients in a cupboard. Learning writing can be like practicing an instrument, but your problem doesn't always present itself like a score. And so on.

****

Choose impossible metaphors.

COMMENTARY: CONSIDER THE SHAPE OF TIME

Set aside the things that you want students to read or look at, the things that are typically thought of as the content of learning, and instead, consider the shape of time, the patterns of activity, the rhythms of return that make up your work. Look at the classes you teach and ask "What are the things I ask my students to do?" Ask yourself, "How do I ask them to spend their time."

Think about what the time you spend tells them about what you think is important. Name that shape, the patterns, the rhythms in your own practice, in your learning, and in the classes you organize and teach. What would you change if you could?

FOUR PRINCIPLES AND A FIFTH

To persuade others, allow yourself to be persuaded

Before I landed at the St. Agnes Center for Reading and Writing, I'd taught my way through New York City's informal adult education system. I taught basic education, literacy instruction, English as Second Language, and GED prep for community organizations, city programs, non-profits, and a community college. My students invariably were older than I, often by decades. Many had raised or were raising families. Most worked full-time jobs. They were Dominican, African-American, Puerto Rican, East and West African, Russian, Bulgarian and Polish, Irish American and Chinese, Jamaican, Haitian, Bajan. The teachers came from various educational backgrounds. Some had BAs or PhDs, and some had master's degrees in English, adult education, or teaching English to speakers of other languages. I met artists and actors, ex-Peace Corps and public school teachers. I met nuns and musicians. In sum, I met some of the most dedicated teachers I've ever met. They were dedicated to the craft of teaching and to the lives of their students, lives upon which learning to read, write, and speak English would have an immediate impact.

The Center was located on the top floor of the St. Agnes Library, between 81st and 82nd Street on Amsterdam in Manhattan. It's a busy branch that served many affluent readers, and its book sale had a reputation that brought lines early in the morning on the first day. There were housing projects further up on Columbus, and the area was still home to working class families on the avenues that went east toward the park and ran north to Harlem. Over the last twenty years, the affluent have driven many long-time residents out and replaced them with college students, graduate students, young professionals, and professional couples raising families. It was a great location for a center. Students and tutors came from the surrounding neighborhoods, but most took advantage of the nearby express and local trains to travel after or before work from other parts of Manhattan

Two professionals, a director and an assistant director, staffed each center. Professional staff recruited students and tutors, trained the tutors, and managed the centers. The St. Agnes Center was an open, well-lit room the size of the entire floor. Ten or twelve round tables with chairs were arranged around the room. There was a small kitchen, an office, and a back room large enough to fit students comfortably along two rows of computers. Five-foot high bookshelves built into walls ran the length of the room on either side of where the students and tutors worked. The Center had a substantial budget for books, so the shelves were filled. One of the most pleasant tasks of the director and assistant director was to maintain the collection. Adult new readers who wander into a library often find themselves reading children's books. But the Center's library was filled with carefully chosen books written for primary and secondary school students. The books were chosen because they might appeal to the students and because they could be easily read and enjoyed. We tried to acquire books that mirrored what students might find in the stacks downstairs. We bought poetry and fiction. Much of the fiction came from publishing houses that produced books for and by adults learning to read, so they had adult themes, but were short books with brief chapters geared for readers at various levels of reading fluency.

I arrived at St. Agnes at the end of a fitful year of frequent staff turnover. Over that year, many students and tutors drifted off until the day program closed, and in the evenings attendance shrank to a core of four tutors and about twenty students. The prescribed whole language curriculum had been lost as tutors and students struggled to create a sense of continuity for themselves and turned to techniques they had experienced or observed outside of the program. Students and tutors had come to rely more and more on spelling tests, memorization, word lists, and reading aloud within groups. One group read through books together the way I remembered from the second grade. Each member took a line or a paragraph. The tutor made corrections when one stalled. Then the group completed spelling tests followed by bits of writing on subjects the students chose, a vestige of the whole language techniques they'd been taught. The students, three women in their sixties, respected the tutor, who came each Tuesday and Thursday directly from a demanding job in a bank, always with good humor and a plan. Whatever I might have thought about the efficacy of the night's work, the students shared a belief that the work had value.

By the time I arrived, a year of rotating staff had led to a low-grade adversarial tension, with program staff on one side and students and their tutors on the other. This tension was complicated by the fact that the whole language curriculum the program advocated struck many of the students and tutors as counterintuitive. Whole language advocates believed that the most effective way to teach reading and writing was to give learners meaningful texts to read and to share with them the tools and processes that "real" writers used. Whole language classrooms gave students time to read and discuss books that mattered to them,, taught them to draft and revise. and turned the classrooms into "writing workshops." Advocates of phonics-based instruction favored systematic instruction in the written representation of the sounds of the English language, carefully programmed to increase the reader/writer's fluency and confidence. Whole language advocates pointed to the work their students produced; advocates of phonics instruction pointed to research that demonstrated the efficacy of phonics and inconclusive findings to support whole language.

At the Centers for Reading and Writing, tutors were taught to use invented spelling with their students. The texts students wrote would be jumping-off points for lists of words to learn and would be "translated" eventually into texts that would be revised and, often, published in a Center journal. Invented spelling represented to many then, as it still does, a serious lapse in pedagogical judgment. For some, invented spelling represented the freedom to write, for others it represented declining standards and an unwillingness to provide learners with common sense instruction in how to spell. Whole language teachers encouraged fluency by inviting students to draft without regard for correctness. The practice stems from the theory that when a new writer or reader has to stop and agonize over a word's spelling, it inhibits her ability to express herself, which in turn makes learning frustrating and unpleasant. If skill and fluency improve with practice, invented spelling enabled students to compose *meaningful texts* and develop them. Learners could draft letters, stories, and poems, which gradually would evolve into clean texts and, on the way to those texts, would extend to other tasks, like working with spelling and phonetics. But this also means texts of two or three sentences in which the only words that appear complete may be articles like *the* or *an*, or coordinating conjunctions like *but* or interspersed blank lines with a letter at the beginning, or clumps of letters, consonants mostly, standing in for the word as the student spoke it aloud or heard it.

But for many of the students and tutors at St. Agnes, the use of invented spelling was simply a stubborn refusal to teach spelling. They'd experienced how embarrassing it was to produce a text that seemed incomprehensible even to sympathetic readers, let alone those strangers who'd be quick to criticize or even ridicule them. To not know how to spell meant to not be understood. But I knew that studying lists of words and writing them ten times—the first three times conscious of each letter, the next three still remembering the word but mostly following the groove, the last four possibly reproducing a misspelling because you don't really need to pay attention to move your hand—would not make them more fluent readers and writers. For the administrators of the Centers, who were trying to implement a difficult curriculum, the efflorescence of spelling tests and reading aloud, along with their dominance of a night's work, represented a program that had completed a slow turn and was now travelling resolutely in the wrong direction.

I also wondered ("knew" is not the right word) whether an emphasis on spelling reinforced something I saw many new readers do. They relied on a limited set of strategies. When they arrived at a word in a book they could not pronounce, they would stop and sound it out, which would turn into a laborious, letter by letter effort, from the first letter to the last. As one of many strategies, "sounding it out" seemed reasonable, but as a primary strategy, students often hewed to it with a conviction that closed off what the context could tell them. Or they believed that reading and writing were synonymous with pronunciation and correct spelling.

Sometimes, you plunge on despite a student's belief that what is being asked of her is useless busywork because it's your job to keep the beat. Who else will keep a student's anxiety from ruling her? Who else but a teacher sees beyond what discourages a student to the success that a little more hard work, work that may seem futile but isn't, will produce? And yet, I also wondered whether my attachment to the idea of "whole language" and "invented spelling" was keeping me from seeing that the students were right, that in fact, I was teaching them in the way I wanted them to learn, rather than responding to their insights about what was missing in what we'd been teaching of St. Agnes.

So, I learned to teach spelling and to teach people how to learn to spell. If I want someone to work in an unfamiliar way, I must accept that she is free to think I'm wrong. The only thing I can ask of a group of learners is to see for themselves and then decide.

Hospitality, an ancient good

The tutors and students came at the end of work days, or before night shifts. Despite the blizzard of print that we live in every day and the regular exhortations to improve one's self or one's circumstances, learning is not central to most people's lives. But I saw that they attended like the devout attend houses of worship. The community they created welcomed and incorporated new members, kept a seat warm for those who came and went, and wove the work of learning into lives through an act of will. And yet I had somehow came into "possession" of a place that existed in the most important way because of them. In a sense, I found myself the owner of the home they occupied.

Whatever tensions might have existed prior to my arrival at St. Agnes, I was treated with hospitality, which is an ancient good. Once I was in their home, I was a guest, and once I was guest, I was received with warmth and respect. They didn't meet me with "Will we or won't we agree and get along?" Their first loyalty was to welcoming a stranger. In time, I was no longer a guest.

Not a class, but a community of shared work

What I found at St. Agnes was, essentially, a Beit Midrash, a House of Study.

The traditional Beit Midrash is a room attached to a synagogue or in a school, filled with texts and tables where they can be studied.

95

Textual study and interpretation is central to traditional Jewish life. Students gather in pairs to study Talmud, the compendium of legal commentaries on the Torah and interpretations of those commentaries that also record the disputes of ancient rabbis who tested and shaped the nature of Jewish Law as it would be understood and re-argued for the next thousand years. The room is full of other books that merit study, other central texts of traditional Jewish life, the study of which prepares the learner to engage both in what it has meant to be a Jew and follow the Law in the world and what it means today. The part of the Talmud known as the Mishnah, or Oral Torah, records the disputes of rabbis, not as third person summaries or critical précis, but as dialogue. The Mishnah doesn't report the dispute as an outcome, but leaves the conversation unresolved. The voices, positions, and players involved are presented without closure. Those who study those arguments later will re-argue the ancient dispute, incorporating later commentary.

I saw a room empty but for tables surrounded by bookshelves. Small group learning structured each evening, but the tutors saw themselves as their students' peers. As much as students were grateful for the tutors' devotion and dedication, the tutors admired and were often in awe of what the students undertook. Since the program was open-ended and grew with the students, learning wasn't built around units or modules or bits of curriculum with beginnings and endings that could be marked; instead, what the students required, in addition to whatever techniques, assignments, or approaches I could provide, was a *way* to work in a place that supported that way. A way to work is a place to come to rest, solid earth under your feet. Some Buddhists I've heard talk about meditation discuss letting your weight go into the ground beneath you; in a sense, knowing that the earth will support your weight, which, weirdly, is not something we all take for granted. And they'll also talk about holding your seat. Buffeted by uncertainty and distraction, the practice of meditation, whatever practice you choose, becomes a simple set of physical and internal movements that enable you to maintain your purpose, to not get up and walk away. What we need to know is not all there is to know, but a way to learn helps make the collaboration a work of its own, so that tutors and tutors feel useful, challenged and fulfilled by their work.

People are more likely to learn some new way if they have the tools to direct their own work

We made changes in the environment to facilitate tutor and student interaction. We used the walls full of bookshelves differently than they had been used. We had books geared toward adult themes but in language accessible to new readers, as well as non-fiction works and other materials written for adults to read, but they had been turned spine in, leaving many shelves half empty and the titles difficult to read. Most of these books were thin with narrow spines, hard to read vertically. We turned the books to face out. The library used inexpensive, mass produced aluminum U-shaped bookends with short, flat, curved feet sticking out on either side to fit under a book and prop it. We slipped a copy of each book over the "U" so it stood up straight, making it inviting and easy to look at.

We set up a wall to display student work. Anything that was ready and prepared was posted for students in other groups to read. We set up regular social events to celebrate student achievement—usually tabulated by the amount of hours students had attended tutoring, a simple way to honor dedication. At the center of the room was a resource table where students stored folders of work from one day to the next, each folder containing drafts of pieces of writing, collections of spelling words and exercises, and lists of books read. Their first task when entering the room was to get their folders, get their coffee, and get to work. The table also held various office supplies—pens, pencils, markers, Post-Its, pads, extra folders, staples, and three-hole punches. We needed, as a center, students and tutors alike, to create some kind of system, a spine for work that insured that each night students would be reading in a reflective and helpful way, focusing on letter sounds and spelling, producing writing motivated by their own goals and desires to speak, and reading for a sustained period of time. So space wasn't the only issue; time was important, too. I divided the night into sections that I asked the tutors to follow uniformly. Because our program relied on a mostly working population of volunteers and students, to give everyone a chance to arrive the first twenty or thirty minutes were devoted to self-directed, silent reading.

The great majority of students and tutors arrived on time, but they often cut it close, and we needed a way to gradually bring the work up to speed without losing instructional time to interruptions and re-explanations of work and lessons. In this way we offered students a quiet time to read, to separate the day's work from the time of learning, to catch up in the coffee room or to check in on some business, and to slowly enter the frame of mind they needed to learn. The rest of the time was divided into periods spent generating new writing and various kinds of "word" work—time for spelling practice, attention to letter/sound combinations, and group projects. The group projects consisted of reading and writing activities that they worked on together. Sometimes it was an area of concern they might have chosen as a group—reading the newspaper, working with advertisements, etc., or activities related to improving their skills. Instead of making it the tutors' responsibility to submit plans, I made it my responsibility to check in with them during tutoring time and to build a way of working with them from night to night, as well as to begin to see the future in longer stretches. I developed a tutoring handbook which I hoped provided some support. I divided it into sections that mirrored the work we wanted them to do, and wrote plans more or less like recipes because they asked for them. I knew these plans wouldn't limit their work, and would provide a secure place from which to depart. I developed tutor training which took place over several weeks that began with investigations of the tutors' own literacy histories, student speakers, visits to groups, practice of techniques and practice lessons. The goal was to create continuity between what they did, saw, and were expected to practice. The congruence between the physical space and time freed students and tutors to focus on the work they came to do and mirrored a way they might read and write at home. They undertook a process full of starts and stops, full of contradictions but, one they powered. Then, a mistake isn't a mistake, it's only part of the way.

Get out of the way

Kabbalists call it *tzimtzum*, the way God contracts and makes space for the world to be born. It may not be that grand, but it's an important truth for a teacher. You can shape the problems and anticipate the obstacles. You can decide what a student encounters and the time it takes. But in the end, you simply must get out of the way, and leave them to do the work of learning. I'm not the first person to suggest that this concept applies to teaching; once it occurred to me, I saw it in many places, and heard speakers use the word to describe virtually the same thing: a teacher has to withdraw to make space for their students' self-creation and learning. I show them models and model process. I build structures to help them on to complex tasks. And then I get out of the way.

Rachmonis

Rachmonis is a Yiddish word that, like *mensch*, translates just a bit and then stops. *Mensch* to Yiddish speakers and Jews who've grown up with the word, suggests a kind of full human being, someone who acts ethically, reliably, and with compassion. My brother, who gave up Thanksgiving with his family to spend a week with me while I recovered on the couch from knee surgery is a mensch. Bernie Madoff is not.

Typically, *rachmonis* translates as compassion. Although I grew up around everyday Yiddishisms, it was Lenny Bruce who introduced me to *rachmonis*. It peppers his live albums, often as a plea—"Have rachmonis, man." Given his suffering, I hear it now like a plea on his own behalf. I understand *rachmonis* to be a kind of compassion from an ethical standpoint, as if when facing the person opposite you, you feel a responsibility to him. It's a detached sort of responsibility sometimes, not driven necessarily by love, but by the conviction that you are connected. The person who faces you deserves regard, recognition, and a measure of relief. What makes it an ethical responsibility is that it's a choice. Rachmonis is a generosity that expects nothing in return, and sometimes expresses itself simply as remaining present with someone who feels that no will have them.

I've described angry and disappointed teachers and inflexible institutions, but that's a partial truth. It would be dishonest to tell the story as if, as I went on, I met teachers who altered my perception of how I belonged because they possessed this quality, *rachmonis*. None of these teachers bent rules or broke them for me. None ever lowered a standard. Most importantly, none lowered an expectation, even when I failed to meet it. But each thought the work I did—learning, writing—was valuable, and took me for myself, along with that work.

These teachers didn't give me pep talks or even reassure me that I had some particular gift. But each had a little *rachmonis* which is fundamental to the work of teaching writing as I understand it. I don't know what choices I would have made had I found school utterly inhospitable, with each point of entry closed. The work that matters most every day in a student's life is the work of great and good teachers. They taught me a basic principle of teaching in general and writing classes in particular, a lesson I was taught over and over again by people who weren't teaching it to me, but acting on it.

COMMENTARY: WHAT PERSISTS

Many years ago I read Steven Berg's book, *In Praise of What Persists.* It's an apt title for a book of interviews with writers because persistence characterizes a successful writer's work. Whether it's yet another draft or yet another rejection, without persistence the poem remains unfinished and unpublished. Few of us finish anything by accident.

I don't remember the interviews well, although I've read many interviews with writers, as many writers and writing teachers will. I remember the title of the book because it's more common to ask "Who persists?" than "What persists?" The latter points me toward what has stayed with me—the values, ideas, principles, or practices I work from; the elemental that guides me when the new, ingenious, and unique have been swept away like leaves on the walk.

So, what persists?

COMMENTARY: ELLEN SCHMIDT

One of the best writing teachers I've ever had is Ellen Schmidt. She teaches a class at her dining room table called "Writing Over the Rough Spots." She's clear that the goal isn't therapeutic, which the name of the class might imply. I've never asked her what it means, exactly, but at her table you'd find someone writing a novel, someone just starting to put words on paper, someone at work on a memoir. The "rough spot" might be a difficult thing in someone's life, but I think Ellen believes that undertaking the work of writing about anything, freely and in the company of people who will listen, can help you write your way through or around that spot. Sometimes the "rough spot" is the rough spot of writing itself—getting started, keeping going, starting again. Another writing teacher whose art I value is the poet and novelist Liz Rosenberg. From time to time I send her a poem, and she writes back with these precise, deft suggestions that always make the work better, and more of what I intended it to be. Bob Stein enabled me to understand my writing difficulties in terms of learning disability, which transformed how I understood myself and what it meant to know how to write. Riv-Ellen Prell taught me a profound lesson about humility through her own actions, which enabled me to see what kind of writer I might want to be, although it took many years to understand that. Louise Wetherbee Phelps read my dissertation with me line by line. I remember the names of many teachers who seemed to appear in my life. I would say that they appeared in my life when it mattered most, but I think it was more that their appearance turned it into a moment that mattered.

****

Name your teachers, in or out of school, and describe what they taught you, whether it was what to do about that last paragraph or how to be patient in the face of the challenges of a new project. Sometimes they don't even know they've taught it to us.

Risk a cliché and list the teachers who made the most difference in your life, your education, your sense of yourself. No, don't do that. Or do that. List the *people* who have made that difference, not in what they did for you (but that also) but in how they regarded you, and what their regard taught you. Try and do this with people you learned from, although you can take them from different settings. Work, the ball field, school, from among your friends. The important thing is to think about people you regarded as teachers, in situations where they might or might not have been defined as a teachers.

Go through each moment, one by one. Ask yourself what it was about that person's actions that helped you learn, and what what it was about your actions that helped you learn.

Tell the story of yourself as a learner as the story of your interaction with each of them along the way.

SOME RULES OF MY THUMB

Talk helps, but try not to talk instead of asking students to write.

Write at every appropriate moment in any available way.

Do the work in class. That way you can answer the questions they need answered as they arise, rather than sending them home to do it the same way they always have.

True, there is no one way to write, but many of your students will have only one way to go about writing, and it helps to show them the many other ways.

Even though there is no single way to write, people typically settle on a way to write, and it usually looks like blank pages and a bunch of other thoughts and pages that grow and change into something they can't take back.

Sometimes products change because we change the process.

Every writing teacher's most compelling flaw is her expertise. Be careful about what you know.

It's not peculiar that often students don't do what we haven't told them, so tell students what they need to know.

How do you decide what they need to know? Ask yourself if not knowing and finding out is the goal, or if knowing and learning something more important is.

Show students what you mean, then let them find out on their own.

Let them find out for themselves, and ask them what they've learned.

Ask them what they've learned, and show them what you meant.

Complex work often depends on a reliable, simple practice, but students often rely on a reliable simple practice and use it to over-simplify complex problems. For some students, a writing process is like using a plane. They use what they know to smooth the edges to make the door fit the doorway, when what they are supposed to do is frame the doorway, then choose the door that fits.

Every once in a while, ask them if they've seen this before.

Remind students where they are and what they are doing.

Treat every student as someone whose work merits the time and attention of the class, despite what they believe about themselves.

Use the blackboard as a notebook and make solving the problems of one person's project something the class can solve together so you can expose what's often hidden about solving writing problems.

When a student offers an idea, rewrite that idea together, see where it goes, choose another, start over.

Make managing the process and the materials a part of the class.

Insist that students take notes on each other's work so they always have a model at hand.

Let students talk to one another about what they intended and how they have succeeded and failed. Have students solve problems together.

There are at least three narratives in a writing classroom: the story of learning to see, the story of learning to create, and the story of learning to talk about what you see and create. There are other stories, too—but there are always these three.

Sometimes, ask for one sentence or idea or solution; sometimes ask for ten. Or three. Or six. First comes the obvious, then the banal and bewildering, then comes the beginning.

Critique always points to the next thing someone makes. It should never end with the deficits of the present work.

When you talk to a student about her work, start with the concrete and move toward the unwritten.

When you talk to a student about her work, start with the unwritten and move toward the concrete. Or start with the concrete and move to the unwritten. Or don't say anything at all.

Don't always ask students to rewrite something because it's weak, but because they can.

If you want someone to learn to "think like," you need to give her a chance to "behave like" for a while. She needs to be in a place that values certain ways of thinking and doing that you trust can help her.

Offer writers the tools and materials they need to solve interesting and meaningful problems, but remember that people sometimes don't know what a tool is for, or even that a thing is a tool, and often they don't know the value of the material they've created, or how to see its value. So, tell them.

SHARE THE RECIPE AND TEACH THE MEAL

Received wisdom since I taught my first writing class in the early 1990s told me to avoid red pens. Red ink discouraged students. Even today I read or hear arguments about the relative merits of green ink, and whether red is just easy to read. For some, word processing programs render the question moot. Teachers enter comments right into a paper.

Writing teachers do have other, better things to do than argue over the psychology of color (red inflames passion; blue calms the spirit, etc.), but the issue was never the ink; it was the metonymy. The red pen stood for an adversarial, almost punitive response to student writing. The teacher corrects rather than responds, and everything is on the block: grammar, punctuation, syntax, organization, the writer's intentions and her powers of expression, so that a student who read the red couldn't decide what, among the many errors she might find herself subject to, she should fix first. Where should she start? What was most important? What would make the most impact? It's been almost three decades since I haven't bothered using a red pen. I opted for cassette tapes and any nearby pen. Do students in my first year writing classes today fear the red pen the way we fear they will? I wonder if trying to explain it to them would be like trying to explain the fuss about legal pot and same sex marriage. But even if they didn't get red ink, the casual humiliations teachers can subject students to through their comments on writing are perennial.

And yet writers sometimes tell a different kind of "red pen" story. I heard Francine Prose tell one. Stephen King includes one in his book about writing. In these stories, the novice writer submits work to a teacher or editor who takes a red pen to it and, with a few arrows and slashes, makes the writing and writer better. As in the red pen story I learned twenty or so years ago, a student or novice faces a teacher or editor. One possesses knowledge and authority, the other submits to it. One reads, the other writes. One speaks and the other listens. The classic anti-red pen story describes the worst kind of response to a student writer, rebuke. The student submits work and waits. The marked-up pages are a monologue.

When Prose and King as young writers face their editors across the desk, they understand themselves to be writers; in fact, they believe themselves to be *good* writers. They expect the editors to be impressed. And this is the lesson of the writer's red pen story. It's the story of a novice who comes to understand something about what the work requires. Sometimes, the writer learns she needs to efface herself. The editor removes the preciousness and flourishes that impressed teachers and schoolmates, but direct a reader's attention to the writer's ingenuity rather than the story. Sometimes, the writer learns to submit to the craft and to turn craft from an unforgiving adversary who polices prose to a *way*. Sometimes she learns what it means to have a voice of her own.

HATS WITHOUT RABBITS

When I was in eighth grade, Mr. Adderton took a chunk of magnesium in a forceps and held it over a Bunsen burner flame until it exploded in a glow. I marveled at the same experiment when my tenth grade chemistry teacher did it, just like my own kid marveled when he saw it in his eighth grade science class.

What did I learn? I learned that magnesium burns at as a relatively low temperature. I learned that one property of magnesium is that science teachers light it to surprise inattentive classes. Although I don't remember the context that prompted the demonstration, I learned that elements have properties. I learned that doing something to something, such as seeing what happens when you put it in the flame of a Bunsen burner, can teach you about its properties, which can reveal its nature. I can't say if this is what Mr. Adderton wanted me to learn, although from what I've learned about doing science since, it strikes me that he wanted us to understand the last part. Harness the average teenager's natural inattentiveness and ignorance to a way to find things out and a reason to find them out, and put him in a place where it matters if she does, and she looks a lot like those English and French scientists in the eighteenth and nineteenth centuries who needed to understand what comprised air or the nature of electricity and magnetism.

What Mr. Adderton did was not a lesson so much as a demonstration. He showed us what happened to magnesium at a certain temperature. Although each of us could have repeated it, we weren't meant to; we already knew how to set things on fire. For those interested in fire, it may have suggested refinements that could reinvest what may have been a waning interest with creative purpose. A demonstration that writing teachers are fond of asks students to rewrite a bit of dialogue for three sharply different audiences. A colleague of mine likes to use a scenario in which his first year college students need to explain what went on the night before to a cop, a friend, and a parent. Like the magnesium demonstration, this activity gets students' attention. In childhood, we learn to how to speak when spoken to by different people in different places; but in adolescence, we make that property of everyday discourse a principle of practice. Yet, like I did when someone lit magnesium for me, students marvel. Ask the next ten people you meet to tell you the atomic formula for water and you'll hear "H2O", even if they don't understand the implications for the water they bathe in and drink. I don't think it's the rhetorical properties per se that hit my friend's students like a table top nova, but the ease with which they find the right style for each audience and the ease with which language responds when the outcome matters and their motives are clear. Writing teachers use this demonstration to launch lessons in rhetorical analysis. "See," this demonstration says, "audience, context, the speaker's motive and purpose, all influence the speaker's speech. You are natural rhetoricians."

Demonstrations make impressions.

Somehow in math and science classes, demonstrations flow naturally into activity: you must see the outcome, you must learn the procedure, you must observe to become expert. But in writing classes, when I rely too much on demonstrations, I find I am exhorting my students to see a thing as I do, which is unpersuasive: that asks students to adopt a belief about writing.

A change in belief makes all the difference when a principle reveals itself to be a good guide. I want to directly address a student's beliefs about style, especially when she chooses a heightened, overly formal style because she imagines it to be the style of experts, when that style actually signals that she is a beginner.

Contrast that lesson with teaching students free or prolific writing, a commonplace technique to share with writing students. Prolific writing is one of those simple, yet difficult techniques that consistent practice makes useful. You choose a period of time and write for that amount of time, say ten minutes. The goal is not really to fill pages, but to fill the time. Although the more regularly you do it, the more text you're likely to produce, the goal is only to write down everything that you think without stopping for that ten minutes. I introduce prolific writing with a lesson that teaches the rules I want them to follow, then spend the rest of class guiding them through five and then ten minute increments. That lesson begins with talk about fluency, about the times that students feel they can't write enough or fill the required pages, about the way an internal editor subverts your intentions when you write and how you can sometimes turn on yourself without knowing it and thwart your best work. I discuss how learning to write, at least once we leave the early primary grades, happens under performance conditions. Almost every time you have an opportunity to write, you're graded. So I ask, how do writers practice? Musicians play scales and work with a piece; bands, dancers and actors rehearse; artists make work that no one ever sees.

I introduce prolific writing as the solution to a problem. I introduce it as a way to practice the simple challenge of getting words on paper and getting started. I introduce it as a way to cultivate a particular frame of mind that a writer can access, a frame of mind that sets the internal editor aside. I introduce it as a tool they can deploy, one that helps them accumulate pages, and one they can use purposefully to explore a specific topic. I introduce it as a practice that can help calm them or give them peace of mind. However I introduce it, it only reveals its value by being used, and only to the extent that a writer feels that it solves a problem.

MAKING THE CLASS

Once again, I sit down to make the class.

It is Saturday, August 24, 2013.

Class begins Tuesday.

I have been working on the class all summer in bits and pieces; have been working on the class for twenty-five years, in a way.

Every time it's time to make the class, the past pours in.

I taught my first writing class in 1986, between my third and last year of college. I came to teach the class by accident. I'd been hired as a peer counselor for an Educational Opportunity Program Summer Program at the college I attended. Newly enrolled students attended for four weeks before starting school in September. They met other students in the program, learned their way around, got a taste of what was to come, found out where they needed to go if they needed a hand. I've taught for comparable programs since. They help.

I and my colleagues Sarah and Vito lived with the students in the dorm, accompanied them places, helped during study hours, ate with them, and scheduled fun. We assisted teachers in their classes. My teacher left the job towards the end of the second week.

Suddenly, I found myself "the teacher."

I did what I still do when I don't know something: I sought the advice of someone I respected and read a book.

Bob Stein gave me a copy of Ponsott and Deen's *Beat Not the Poor Desk,* which I still reread a bit at a time each year. Their book, *The Common Sense: What to Write, How to Write It and Why* sits right there, at ten o'clock. When I am through here, when I go back to planning the class, I'll take another look.

He also gave me a copy of a document he'd made and shared with colleagues, a list of theses on teaching writing, which I carried for many years until I lost it. Year by year, it seemed to become more and more true, until, I suppose, it disappeared into my own practice. I lost it because I remembered it.

His help helped, but I still didn't know what to do on Monday. That was my most important consideration at the time: *What would we do?*

I've pieced together how we spent the next couple of weeks. I believe I taught them how to free write, and we spent time doing that in class.

I had the notion that I wanted to demonstrate to them something about language. I wrote Lewis Carroll's "Jabberwocky" on the board. We spent a class period reading and making sense of it, or making sense of the way it could be made sense of, or why it could be made sense of. I remember I asked them to compose directions from one place to another, from the dorm to class, from home to a place in their neighborhood, with two audiences in mind, native and stranger.

I suppose we also talked a lot. While I taught them, I still worked as peer counselor and continued to live, eat, and spend time outside of class with them. It's possible we talked more pointedly about school and school writing, where they came from and what they expected to find because I knew them first as a counselor. I'm not certain, although I remember that, on the whole, I came to believe quite quickly that the people they needed to talk to most were each other, until they needed to talk to me, at which point, I learned, I needed to listen. *To listen.* There's a lesson I forget and learn over and over again.

When the program ended, I saw very little of the students in it. Some returned in September; others didn't. Family, finances, or fear stepped in. Some had obligations they could not renege on, and tried a college closer to home. I'd pass those who'd returned and say hello, but the program had done its work. They became a close-knit group, relied on each other, and used the resources of the EOP office when they needed them. They were first-year students and I was a senior. Our paths were separate.

I thought of this class over the next few years as a benchmark, a past problem to reconsider as I learned more about teaching. I concluded that I'd done a generally poor job.

About five or six years later, I was walking up Broadway in Manhattan. I know exactly where I was; I was approaching West Side Judaica, between 88th and 89th street. A gray fall day, big bag of papers and books slung across my body, banging my hip.

Out of the crowd, coming my way, was Bernard. He walks up to me and says, "Thank you for the class. I learned a lot."

Sometimes, despite all the teaching, students learn.

IMAGINE THE FOLLOWING

You are on a journey.

You bring along knowledge and skills about how to make fire and build a shelter, find food, cultivate the soil, and use plants to make medicine. Many of the things you'll need to survive, you'll find on the way.

Part of the path you walk is mapped. You know that a map is only as good as the person who drew it. Much may have changed. You are constantly aware of the discrepancy between the way the map reads and what you observe. You note the differences for the way back.

A purpose defines your journey: future settlement. Thus, you have concerns: fertile land, proximity to water, wildlife, the presence of others. Other factors define your journey, including the knowledge and experience you bring, your memories, your feeling for place.

You note that while some plants are familiar, others seem different: hypotheses emerge, experiments form in your mind. Old crafts may be useful, may be impractical. You store knowledge of plants and herbs, wildlife, rock formations, soil. You compose love poetry that uses new names in old forms. You rehearse the tale you tell when your return for the others. You adjust old ideas to new information and reconfirm previously held convictions.

Mentally, the physical journey takes shape. In fact, this physical journey comprises several mental journeys. You shape the mass of data that filters through your senses according to your identity, purpose, and experience.

The way home is a different journey entirely. Gathered into landmarks and places you've been before, your mental map makes it seem shorter and more direct. Your familiarity with these landmarks doesn't diminish the incidence of surprise. They seem more astonishing now that they are set in the background of a world you remember.

When you return, you must recount what you've found. You craft a journey for others to take. You must shape your already shaped journey in the minds of others. You will have evidence: maps, seeds and petals pressed between pages, testimony of dreams dreamed with your head against a stone pillow.

When they retake your journey, it will be without you as a guide. You give them your journey like an apple: they can eat it and plant the seeds later, elsewhere, in new soil.

Whatever they need to find, they will find on their way. But they bring with them knowledge and skills—

The boy was playing one afternoon
when an ill and exhausted man stumbled in
the courtyard. He called to his parents and the three—
his father, his mother, and himself—brought the man into their home
Then put him to bed. When the man woke the next morning
he explained, "I am the king's messenger." He showed
the pouch he carried, its silver seal and its eleven silk knots,
elaborately tied, which no one but the royal knotsmsith could loosen.
"I must bring the pouch to the Quadrennial Capital,
where the King spends every fourth year.
It's taken almost the entire four years to reach it.
It is only a few miles. Can your boy take it for me?"

His parents agreed. The boy had shown little aptitude for anything
but pitching a ball he'd made out of rags against the courtyard wall,
which is what he was doing the messenger arrived.
So they found him a blue shirt and pants, something like the messenger's
    uniform,
slung the pouch over his shoulder, knotted the messenger's sash
so it would fit, and waved to him from the courtyard arch
and pointed toward the Capital Road. However,
though the Quadrennial Capital was near, the way was long.
Barbed wire; closed borders, avalanche and flood.
It was three years until he reached a city he could see if he stood on
    his parent's roof.

The Capital, built on a promontory, rose from the mountains around it.
Over the years the boy,
now a messenger, worked his way toward it.
Some months it shadowed him to his left, others to his right.
As he grew close, it disappeared into the carved rock,
then, suddenly, all he saw was the city's wide walls.
They curved in either direction, punctuated by arches in the dark stone.
He chose one arch and entered.
It was not dark and not empty,
but full of others like himself, shuffling through the great tunnel into
    the city.
Lamps hung from the walls suspended from chains.
Sooty smoke streaked the ceiling.
He entered the city one year before the King.
For the next 364 days he slept in parks.

He found work as a night guard at the entrance he entered through.
Since he already owned a uniform, he was hired on the spot.
His job was to wait for the Messiah and ring the bell if he came.
On the 364th night he quit his job and found a tree near the castle,
propped his head on a root that knuckled out of the turf,
turned the sash and pouch like a pillow,
and slept.
He meant to sleep lightly, so he wouldn't miss his turn at the castle
    gate
but fell asleep right away.
In his dreams, he stares down at a crown.
The crown is the Capital's image.
It teems with entrances and exits, rivers and girders,

tiny stoves and set tables
seen through small windows with folds of curtain tied back.
Picnic meals in parks, cups on café tables
as if those who left them would return soon.
The boy lifts it, lowers it on his head.
He is surprised to find it is light.
Light! He woke like a fly snatched from midair.
The boy stood quickly and gathered his sash and pouch,
which he threw over his shoulder, then ran through closing doors.
At the end of the long hallways was another door.
He raced for it, burst through it and found himself face to face
with a tired man putting on a gold crown.

Light, the goldsmith thought, feeling the crown weight on his head.
He'd *tried* to make it light, beating and thinning the gold,
but the scale—he thought it would break a man's neck.
When they brought him here, what, seven years ago.
The guards told him to use his own head for measure.
At night, he slept in a locked room beside the workroom.
He hadn't seen his family, though he received their letters—
saw that the King, as promised, had provided for them.

When the boy burst into the room, his clothes nearly rags,
the goldsmith still wore the crown.
"Sire," the boy said, and dropped to a knee.
"Stand," the goldsmith said.
The boy rose and handed the goldsmith the pouch,
which the goldsmith set on his work table, unopened.
Then he removed the crown, and set it over the pouch.
"But," said the boy, "your message."
"You are the message," the goldsmith said. "Tell me everything."
He put his arm around the boy and led him back the way he'd come,
through the now unlocked door, down a long unfamiliar hall,
into the daylight. It felt like noon, the goldsmith thought.
"Now," he said, "Let's walk."

As soon as they reached the street, the goldsmith knew he was lost.
"Listen," he said, "I've left my glasses behind."
He patted his pockets. "Could you lead me?"
"I'm sorry, Your Highness," said the boy, "I only know the way I
    came."
"Since you've already reached where you're going, what other way is
    there?"
The boy told the story of how he came to be a messenger,
and how long it had taken him to reach the castle with the message.
The goldsmith apologized for asking so much of him.
The boy told him he was proud to have done something for the King,
"Even if all I have to offer is a gift for waiting."
"You have many more gifts than that.
You'll learn the names later," said the goldsmith.

They crossed a narrow bridge which ended in a road
that branched into other roads the boy had taken at one time or another.
Within a few hours, they were at the boy's home.
The goldsmith drew a hand full of gold shavings out of his pocket
he'd been ferreting away for escape home
and pressed them on the boy. "Would you like to come in and rest,
    sire?"
"Nah," said the goldsmith. "Gotta go."
The boy entered the courtyard, where his mother and father met him.
They recognized him immediately, though he was taller.
It took the goldsmith a year to reach home,
but when he did,
his family left their work and ran out to meet him.

WORKS CONSULTED AND RELIED UPON

Throughout this book, I indicate where I relied on a scholar or writer's specific concepts and language but writing teachers are pack rats and mockingbirds. We collect and build out of what we collect. Ideas and concepts circulate. I am always looking for ways to articulate what I see emerging in my classes and I also look for work that challenges what I've come to believe. Below is a list of books and authors I refer to in the book, but it also includes work that unmistakably shaped how I express what what writing classrooms have taught me. I have another reason for including this list in this way. I was trained in a tradition that encouraged teachers to see classrooms as laboratories and themselves as artists, intellectuals and researchers. I was taught to observe students closely, to the work that they turned in as data that would help me teach more effectively. I learned to read widely, to draw on anything that could help me answer the questions, "What does it mean to know how to write? What does it mean to learn? How should I teach?" For instance, I believe my work became much richer when I began to look at how psychologists understood creativity, what philosophers had to say about the nature of knowledge, how mathematicians understood discovery and how math teachers taught students to solve problems. I didn't use a method of inquiry or research of the kind a PhD program might teach and scholarship expects, although I rely on the discoveries that others make using those methods. My reason for writing this book in the way I've written it is to offer teachers a way to investigate what they know and what they teach their students. Whatever means you have for expressing what you understand, meditating on what puzzles you,and investigating the questions that possess you, use them. Teachers, in their way, have always been practical philosophers of knowledge. The books below helped me do that work. It was a curriculum constructed along the way, and I'm indebted to the people whose work I read, as well as the colleagues who shared their thoughts me and teachers who pointed me in a direction that, whether it was the right or wrong one, either opened a door, or reassured me that it was okay to close one.

Aristotle. (1986). *Nicomachean ethics* (pp. 364–375). New York, NY: Penguin Classics, 2003.

Connell, W. M., Sheridan, K., & Gardner, H. (2003). On abilities and domains. In R. Sternberg (Ed.), *Psychology of abilities, competencies and expertise* (pp. 126–155). New York, NY: CUP.

Dalmiya, V., & Linda. A. (1993). Are 'old wives tales' justified? In A. Linda & P. Elizabeth (Eds.), *Feminist epistemologies* (pp. 217–244). New York, NY: Routledge.

Eisner, E. (1982). *Cognition and curriculum: A basis for deciding what to teach and how to evaluate it.* New York, NY: Longman Group.

Eisner, E. W. (2002/2005, September 29). What can eduction learn from the arts about the practice of education? In M. K. Smith (Ed.), *The encyclopedia of informal education (Infed).* London, UK: YMCA George Williams College. Retrieved March 31, 2010 from www.infed.org/biblio/eisner_arts_and_the_practice_or_education.htm

Goodman, N. (1978). *Ways of worldmaking.* Indianapolis, IN: Hackett.

Goodman, N. (1984). *Of mind and other matters.* Cambridge, MA: Harvard University Press.

Kaufer, D. S., & Butler, B. S. (1996). *Rhetoric and the arts of design.* Mahwah, NJ: Lawrence Erlbaum Associates.

Keinänen, M., Kimberly, S., & Howard, G. (2003). Opening up creativity: The lenses of axis and focus. *Creativity and reason in cognitive development* (pp. 202–220). Cambridge, MA: Cambridge University Press.

Lauer, J. (1970). Heuristics and composition. *College Composition and Communication, 21*(5), 396–404.

Morenberg, M. (2002). *Doing grammar* (3rd ed). Oxford: Oxford University Press.

Palmo, J. T. (2011). *Into the heart of life.* Ithaca, NY: Snow Lion Publications.

Perkins, D. (1997). What is understanding. In *Teaching for understanding: Linking research with practice* (pp. 39–47). San Francisco, CA: Jossey-Bass Education Series.

Perkins, D. N., Jay, E., & Tishman, S. (1993). Beyond abilities: A dispositional theory of thinking. *Merrill Palmer Quarterly, 39*(1), 1–21.

Phelps, L. W. (1991). Literacy and the myth of the natural attitude. In *Composition as a human science* (pp. 108–131). New York, NY: Oxford University Press.

Polanyi, M. (1962). *Personal knowledge: Towards a post critical philosophy.* Chicago, IL: University of Chicago Press.

Polya, G. (1973). *How to solve it: A new aspect of mathematical method.* Princeton, NJ: Princeton University Press.

Ponsot, M., & Rosemary, D. (1982). *Beat not the poor desk.* Upper Montclair, New Jersey: Boynton.

Ruddick, S. (1995). *Maternal thinking: Towards a politics of peace.* New York, NY: Beacon Press.

Ryle, G. (1949). *Concept of mind.* New York, NY: Barnes and Noble Books.

Scheffler, I. (1990). In *Praise of the cognitive emotions*. New York, NY: Routledge.

Schon, D. A. (1990). *Educating the reflective practitioner: Toward a new design for teaching and tearning in the professions*. San Francisco, CA: Jossey-Bass Publishers.

Snyder, G. (1979). Interview. In R. Gibbons (Ed.), *The poet's work: Twenty nine poets on the origins and practice of their art*. Chicago, IL: University of Chicago.

Star, J. R. (2005). Reconceptualizing procedural knowledge. *Journal for Research in Mathematics Education, 36*(5), 404–11.

Sterelny, K. (2003). *Thought in a hostile world: The evolution of human cognition*. Oxford: Oxford University Press.

Sudnow, D. (1979). *Talk's body*. New York, NY: Knopf.

Tishman, S., Jay, E., & Perkins, D. N. (1993, Summer). Teaching thinking dispositions: From transmission to enculturation. *Theory Into Practice, 32*(3), 147–53. Print.

Varela, F. (1999). *Ethical know-how: Action, wisdom and cognition*. Stanford, CA: Stanford University Press.

Winner, E., Hetland, L., Veenema, S., Sheridan, K., & Palmer, P. (2006). Studio thinking: How visual arts teaching can promote disciplined habits of mind. *New directions in creativity, aesthetics, and the arts*. Boston, MA: Harvard University Project Zero, Harvard Graduate School of Education. Retrieved from http://halifaxvisualartsstudio.wikispaces.com/file/view/StudioThinking.pdf

Printed in the United States
By Bookmasters